Research Your
Family Tree

This is a Parragon Book
First published in 2002

Parragon
Queen Street House
4 Queen Street
Bath BA1 1HE, UK

ISBN: 0-75258-259-3

A copy of the CIP data for this book is available from the British Library upon
request.

The right of Fiona Screen to be identified as the author of this work has been
asserted in accordance with Section 77 of the Copyright, Designs and Patents Act
of 1988.

Editorial, design and layout by Essential Books, 7 Stucley Place,
London NW1 8NS

Printed and bound in China

Birth and marriage certificates on pages 58, 61 and 74: Office for National Statistics © Crown
copyright. Reproduced with the permission of thr Controller of Her Majesty's Staionery Office.

Research Your Family Tree

Fiona Screen

Contents

Introduction

Researching your family tree (or genealogy, to use its more technical name) has exerted an enduring fascination over generations of families. Its popularity as a hobby, or rather a lifetime's quest, continues to rise.

Once you start on the genealogical trail, you'll soon find that you're not alone. Everybody's doing it – or at least knows someone who's doing it. It's not difficult to understand why the subject proves so intriguing, and the research so addictive. We all have a natural interest in finding out about what the lives of our ancestors were like and what sort of social and economic circumstances they lived in. And then there's the possibility of finding famous or noble relations, which for some people is the initial motivation behind their research.

Of course everyone likes to boast that his or her ancestors 'came over with William the Conqueror from Normandy' (I have a document myself in my grandmother's handwriting claiming to illustrate exactly this). Gasps of amazement are meant to ensue. In reality, it's not such a great claim, as thousands of us will be related to the group that settled on these shores in 1066. In fact, some genealogists have said that in a room of 100 people, around 80 will be descended in some way from Edward III – this is based on taking the known number of Edward's descendants from some centuries ago, and calculating their notional rate of increase.

There are entire books devoted to the subject of finding royalty in your family. If that's your starting point, fine. But there's a lot more to researching your family tree than that. You'll probably find that as the fascination of the subject takes over and you become more and more absorbed in your findings, your original reason may well fade into the background as you become more familiar with the family members you are discovering.

People may become interested in their family tree for a number of different reasons. The most common are an unusual surname, the quest for noble or famous ancestors, as mentioned, the desire to find out whether an anecdote or story passed down through the family has any truth in it, and the desire to carry on the work started by a relation who has passed away.

If you do have an unusual surname, as I do, you should find your research easier. (You'll also find it's not quite as unusual as you thought). If, on the other hand, you are one of the Smiths and Joneses of this world, then brace yourself, you have a long journey ahead. Don't be put off though. There's no reason why you cannot successfully research a very common surname, as long as you know how to use the sources available in the most efficient way, and are blessed with a considerable amount of patience and perseverance.

Often genealogy is a pursuit taken up in retirement, as it can be fairly time-consuming, though increasingly people of all ages are becoming interested in the subject. There really is no way of saying how much of your time your family tree research will take, because it is not something that has a beginning, a middle and an end. Even if you reach an impasse researching one particular ancestral line (sometimes known as a 'pedigree'), there will always be many other branches of your family you can follow. You can certainly research back several generations in the space of a few months, and this can be quite satisfying in itself if you want to concentrate on your closest ancestors, for which information will be more readily available, and build up a real picture of them and their lives. If you want to go back further, it's basically a never-ending story.

A word on surnames

People often think that understanding the origin of a particular name is key to being able to create a family tree. Surnames are a fascinating subject and it's true that genealogy is only possible because of the handing down of surnames from the thirteenth and fourteenth centuries. However, just because your name is Baker and you believe your ancestors were bakers by trade, this does not get you very far in terms of genealogy. There will have been hundreds of other bakers around,

even in the Middle Ages. If not related to a profession, surnames tend to denote a particular geographic area. This is where surnames can be more helpful in tracing ancestors – if your name is Ashton, then at some point your ancestors will have been living in one of the various places called Ashton in this country.

At least 50 per cent of medieval surnames were related to a geographic location, others were patronymic (from father to son, such as Williamson, Rowlandson), from nicknames (Short, Redhead) or denoted foreign origin (Beecham from Beauchamp). You should also bear in mind that through the ages people have always had a fondness for changing their names, both surname and forename. You have no guarantee that the name you have been given did not change at some point on your ancestral line.

About this book

This book is a beginner's guide to researching your family tree and is intended for those with little or no knowledge of the subject. It will tell you about the main sources of information in England and Wales, how to go about your initial research, describe what the Internet can offer the amateur geneaologist, and show you how a family tree can be drawn.

I will be concentrating on the main registers of births, marriages and deaths held at the Family Records Centre (FRC), which date from 1832, and also those held in parish registers, which enable you to take your research further back. There is not the space in here to cover the many more specialized sources of information that are dealt with in detail by some of the huge comprehensive tomes devoted to genealogy, but this book will point you in the right direction if you do want to follow these trails.

Similarly, this book is only international in that it deals with Internet research. In the main we are looking at the records for England and Wales only. If you know that your grandfather was Austrian, then only your family's personal records will help you research his

ancestral line in this country. This book, however, will give you some helpful guidelines if you wish to pursue international sources, particularly in Chapter 7, which covers family tree research on the Internet.

CHAPTER 1

PREPARATION

Get organized

Organization is everything in genealogy. When researching your family tree, you will be making a lot of notes and drawing on many different sources. If you don't want to get buried under piles of paper, with scribbles that must have meant something at the time but now are little short of gibberish, then you need to adopt a simple and logical filing system, and discipline yourself to stick with it. Follow these five rules and you'll avoid a lot of timewasting and frustration.

Write everything down. Don't fall into the trap of believing that you can rely on memory – either your own or other people's. This is particularly important when talking to relatives, as it can be easy to get swept along with the narrative of a story. In fact, you may find it awkward, or even impolite, if you have to keep asking a relative to pause, slow down or repeat. Pausing every five minutes for a recap can work well, as this gives you the opportunity to take notes as you hear the facts once again.

Of course the best method of recording conversations is by using a dictaphone. Make sure you ask for clarification of any unusual spellings, as playing back your recordings will not help you with this, and you won't want to bother relatives with phone calls afterwards. Similarly, when you are visiting a record office, library, parish church, graveyard or other source of genealogical information, you should write down absolutely everything you find out.

Write clearly. Don't think your handwriting doesn't matter because you're the only one who needs to read it. Imagine the frustration of travelling half way across the country to find a key piece of missing information, then being unable to decipher what you have written when, three months later, you go back to your notes.

Don't abbreviate. When you are drawing up your family tree there are certain standard abbreviations that are absolutely essential, because of space concerns (see Chapter 8). The family tree simply could not be displayed successfully without them. However, in your own notes abbreviations should be avoided, unless you accompany them with a key. When you have a large amount of material to record it can be very tempting to devise your own system of abbreviation, but this can often be fatal. Referring to relatives by their initials is particularly risky. If you look back through your ancestral line and you're sure to find relations with the same initials, particularly as you go further back, when sons often took their father's forename. Don't make life difficult for yourself.

Develop a logical and efficient filing system.
There are a number of ways you can organize your research material. A good method is to have one loose-leaf file that records pedigrees (family trees or sections of trees), arranged in reverse chronological order, and a second loose-leaf file that has separate pages for individuals, where more detailed information about their life is recorded. The entry for a particular individual on the pedigree file should then cross-refer to the more detailed file. It's often best to work with sections of trees, or mini trees, rather than entire lines, as this makes the information more digestible and you avoid a situation whereby you have a pedigree with many blanks.

A third file could be reserved for fairly sketchy information, which is not yet full enough to be transferred to a family tree or section of a tree. Copies of birth, marriage and death certificates, as well as any other official records, should be kept flat in clear plastic folders, or in special certificate holders. The Family Records Centre (see Chapter 3) has such holders for sale in its shop.

Distinguish between confirmed information and unconfirmed. At any given stage in your research the information you have about your family will be a mixture of that which is known to be fact, and that about which more research is required. The incomplete information may become fact at a later date, or may never be conclusively confirmed. Two good ways of dealing with these different types of information in your notes are: a) to record all unconfirmed information in pencil; or b) to use square brackets. The advantage of pencil is that once you do find the confirmation you are looking for, you can easily rub it out and transfer the entry to pen.

Of course the above five rules presume that you are conducting all of your notetaking on paper. Electronic notetaking has obvious advantages over paper, but comes with its own practical limitations. A laptop, palmtop or phone with inbuilt computer can be incredibly useful for making notes when talking to relatives, but you need to ensure that you are sensitive to the feelings of the people you are talking to, and not just treat it as a research exercise. Relatives might be put off by this technology, which is quite probably alien to them, and by the sight of you tapping away, staring at your keyboard when they are sharing intimate memories with you that may well be difficult to talk about. If you don't know the relative well, then it's probably best to avoid electronic notetaking. Remember these are real people, talking about real lives.

Electronic notetaking in records offices and libraries can work very well, however, particularly if you are a fast and accurate typist. Make sure you carefully read over what you have typed if you want to avoid another unwanted trip to the record office. In other locations, such as churches, electronic notetaking may be completely inappropriate. Find out what the accepted practice is (the Family Records Centre asks all users to turn off mobile phones when they enter, for example), and always be sensitive to your surroundings.

Memories, as mentioned above, cannot be relied on. And yet they form the basis of family-tree research. This is one of the great ironies of genealogy, yet also what makes it so fascinating. You can get a long way checking facts, but genealogy will never be a science in the true sense of the word. When talking to relations about ancestors, start from a position of mistrust. Carefully note down everything you are told, then ask again later, perhaps wording your questions in a different way, to make sure the information tallies. Then if you can, talk to another relative about the same ancestors and see what information they give. Get as full a picture as you can before you go on to confirm everything against the official sources.

Understanding relationships

Few of us will have much trouble grasping the meaning of 'mother', 'father', 'brother', 'sister', 'son', 'daughter', 'grandmother', 'grandfather', 'grandson' or 'grand-daughter'. Similarly, 'aunt', 'uncle', 'cousin', 'niece' and 'nephew' rarely pose a problem. It's when you come to great-aunts, great-grandparents and second cousins twice removed that things start looking more tricky.

- A great-grandparent is your grandparent's parent, or your mother or father's grandparent.
- A great-aunt or great-uncle is a sister or brother of your grandparent.
- A great-great-aunt or great-great-uncle is a sister or brother of your great-grandparent.

There is sometime confusion between 'step' and 'half' relations. If Anne's father dies and her mother Maria marries John, then John is Anne's stepfather. If John already has children, these become Anne's step-brothers and sisters. If, though, Maria and John then have children together, these become Anne's half brothers and sisters. The 'step' means there is no blood relation, just a link by marriage. The 'half' means they have one parent in common. Your in-laws similarly have no blood tie, only a link by marriage (mother-in-law, father-in-law, sister-in-law, brother-in-law, son-in-law, daughter-in-law).

The different types of cousin relationship need some explanation. The children of two siblings are called first cousins (my mother's sister's children are my cousins). Easy enough. The children of two first cousins are then the second cousins of each other. The key to understanding the type of cousin in question is the number of generations there are between you and the common relation. If there is one generation between you and the common ancestor, you are first cousins; if the common relation is two generations away you are second cousins. In other words, first cousins have a grandparent in common, second cousins have a great-grandparent in common.

Cousins are described as 'removed' when they are not of the same generation. This is best shown by the diagram on page 22. You can work out whether a cousin is once, twice or more removed by counting the number of generations between you and the common ancestor (say two) and between your cousin and the common ancestor (say one). The smallest of these numbers determines whether you are first, second or third cousins, and the difference in the generations between you and your cousin determines whether they are once removed, twice removed, etc.

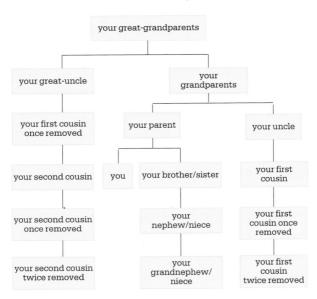

Choose your line

Before you start investigating your family tree, you need to decide which ancestral line you are going to follow. It's important to focus on one line and see this through until you reach a dead end, rather than constantly going off at tangents and researching the line of an aunt or other relation. You can do this later, if you have the time and the inclination.

It's not realistic to think you are going to be able to research a large number of different lines simultaneously. It will become too complicated and you'll end up with lots of bits of information and no real focus to your research. There are practical considerations too. If you are investigating a large number of ancestors, it can be costly, as your research will invariably involve visiting different parts of the country to talk to family members, visit local records offices, check parish records and visit gravestones. Often visits will involve overnight stays.

I'm not saying you shouldn't follow your natural instincts if you become interested in a particular individual as you research your first line and want to find out more about that person. I simply mean that you need to be organized if you don't want to get tied up in knots and dedicate your entire life to nothing but family tree research. Researching just the one line can be quite complex in itself.

The overriding rule when choosing which line to research is to go with whichever one you feel most excited about. A lot of people decide to research a particular family line because of what they already know about that branch of the family. Perhaps you remember tales of a colourful family character from when you were little and are intrigued to know more. Or it could be that, like many people, you have an unusual surname and hope to find out its origins. If so, you will be interested in contacting a 'one-name society'. These are discussed in Chapter 5.

There are important practical considerations to which you should give due thought before embarking on your research. It is far easier and less costly to research an unusual surname. If you know your four grandparents then it's good to concentrate on the family closest to your home. Once you start your research, you'll appreciate being within easy reach of the local records office and public library. If going as far back in time as possible is important to you, then if you know of an ancestor whose surname is that of a parish, village or town, you should go for that name. This means you have a chance of being able to trace the name back to the Middle Ages.

CHAPTER 2

TALKING TO RELATIVES

People new to family-tree research sometimes make the mistake of taking endless trips to records offices, when in fact much of the information they are looking for can be found much closer to home. For any family-tree researcher the golden rule is 'Go with what you know'.

Chapter 3 will tell you all about searching official records of births, marriages and deaths held at the Family Records Centre in London and in local records offices and libraries. Meanwhile, don't plunge into the official records before you have found everything you can from your existing family and extended family. This will not only save you several unnecessary trips to the records offices (and for those outside London this is a particularly important consideration), it will help bring your research to life and make it a meaningful and enjoyable experience. After all, you will learn far more from talking to people who actually knew the ancestors you are researching than from going through hefty indexes for an entry among millions.

Many families pass down birth, marriage and death certificates as well as wills, letters and photographs through the generations. When investigating my own family I was delighted to find that my father had a virtually complete set of birth, marriage and death certificates going back four generations. These had been passed down from parents to children, all perfectly preserved and organized.

As your research progresses, of course, you'll need to consult both the information you have from relatives and the official records, not only to fill in facts you have not been able to find from talking to family members, but also to check that what they have passed on is accurate.

One of your first questions should be 'Has anyone done it before?' The answer is so often yes! During my own research I lost count of the number of times I heard people say, 'Oh yes, so and so started doing ours a few years back …', the keyword here being 'started'. Started then gave up because they didn't really have the time, got distracted by something else, hit a stumbling block and didn't have the motivation to try to negotiate it.

If this is the case then you should seek out the relation who has started the research, as they will be able to give you the benefit of their knowledge and tips on avoiding any pitfalls they may have encountered. Then you can take the research forward yourself. If a relation really has completed comprehensive research on the particular branch you were interested in, then you should try another line. Your ancestors may even have published their research, or perhaps been contacted by others who were publishing their research. The Internet is a good place to search for such publications. The Family Records Centre bookshop is also a mine of information.

Think about what you know first. This may seem a fairly obvious statement, but it's amazing how little you realize you know until you have a reason to think about it. When I started talking to my parents about our family I discovered there were a number of relations, particularly my two great-aunts whom I visited when I was at primary school, that I had completely forgotten about. Gradually (and I mean over a few days rather than a few minutes) their faces came into focus and I found it quite incredible that they had been so deeply buried in my memory. I simply had had no reason to think about them.

Memories resurface gradually. Write down the names of every ancestor you can remember, together with specific details about them, and return to your list a week later. You'll probably be able to add some fresh names, or at least descriptions. From this you can start to build your own mini tree. When you visit relations, get them to check your information (it's a good idea to start in pencil then transfer to ink once you have had the details verified by a relation).

Contacting relations

It may be that you come from a fairly close-knit family where several generations live within the same geographical area. If so, it is likely you will know your grandparents, great-aunts and uncles, for example, reasonably well. It is equally possible that you won't know them at all, that your name may be familiar to them – perhaps not even that.

If this is the case, you need to be sensitive when contacting and visiting them. Turning up out of the blue announcing yourself to be a long-lost second cousin doing family-tree research may seem like a good idea but could set your research off on a really bad footing. Elderly relatives in particular may be made nervous. Or simply not believe you. The best way to approach contacting relatives is to introduce yourself by letter beforehand, preferably by way of an informal CV. This will enable them to place you in an overall picture of the family (if they can think 'Ah yes, this is Michael's sister's daughter', for example) and bring you to life as a person, without any question of a threat. You could include the following:

- Your name, age and address
- Your occupation
- Name of your spouse if you are married, and children if you have them
- Explanation of your relationship to other family members
- Details of your interests, hobbies, previous jobs
- A photograph of you and your family
- If you have met the relation when you were little, a photograph of you from that time, if you have one
- The reasons why you are researching the family tree and if you have contacted any other relatives already
- A diagram of your family tree if you have started it – this should get them interested, particularly if they see blanks they know they can help you fill in.

Make your letter informative but chatty. Avoid making any assumptions about them in it, but say what you *think* you know or remember about them. Letters are preferable to phone calls. Let them know that if they have any family birth, marriage or death certificates these would be extremely useful to you as they will be the bread and butter of your research. Try to find out if they have any other memorabilia that has been passed down through the generations and that could help you build a clearer picture of your family.

It's important to let relatives know you are doing serious research and are not hoping to uncover a family scandal or discover a goldmine. 'There's no money, you know' can be a common reaction. You need to reassure relatives that your motives are completely above board. This should put you in a good position to make the visit as rewarding an experience as possible and will help you best exploit the knowledge that your relation has.

Personal recollections

Recording the personal memories of your relations is absolutely essential to your research and, again, you should exploit this to the full before wasting time searching in the official records. Generally speaking, female members of the family seem to have broader and more accurate memories than the males. I don't know if there is any scientific evidence to back this up, but it certainly seems to be the case that women are a mine of information – grandmothers are particularly good – whereas men can be unreliable. This could well be because your aunts, grandmothers, great-aunts are from a generation when women generally did not work outside the home, and therefore tended to have more social interaction with the rest of the family.

You must be absolutely meticulous in your recording of personal recollections (see Chapter 1) and develop an efficient method of note-taking.

Of course memories are not facts. Information is often passed down through the generations in a fairly random way and, particularly as relations get older, memories can become blurred. Memory is also notoriously selective, and not just in the elderly.

You might assume that yours is a pretty ordinary, straight-down-the-line sort of family, but nearly every family-tree researcher finds some skeletons in the closet at some point. Today we are fairly used to couples having children and opting not to marry, but illegitimacy is far from a modern phenomenon. It happened throughout history. The difference is that for your older relations it was probably a far greater taboo than it is today. If a relative was aware that, say, your grandparents were not married when they gave birth to your parents, they may not pass this information on to you, either because they are uncomfortable with this truth themselves, or because they feel it may upset you. You shouldn't assume that older relations have adopted the moral values of the present day; generally speaking they have not, their values are they ones they grew up with as children.

Issues of illegitimacy, criminality, bigamy, etc. are directly linked to memory. If a family truth has been covered up, then a relation may simply not remember it, or may choose to lie. You should be aware of this when you are doing your research, but be sensitive to the feelings and values of your family and do not put them in a position likely to upset them when this is not necessary. If you do uncover some contentious information, think twice before sharing it with your relations. If they would be genuinely interested to find out that great-uncle John had four different wives at the same time then fine. If not, keep it to yourself.

Memory also has a habit of changing names, occupations, addresses, even physical descriptions. You should always check the information a relative has given you against that of other relations, and against the official sources. Anecdotes are great fun, but often unreliable.

A postal visit

Visiting a relative in person is always the best way of conducting your research, but there will be occasions when lack of time or money mean this is simply not a practical solution; for example, if a relative has moved abroad. In such cases your best bet is to interview by way of a postal questionnaire.

Make sure you write them an initial letter to introduce yourself if you don't know them already. This will break the ice before you approach them with the questionnaire, which can, simply because of the way it is laid out, seem quite formal. You may want to handwrite your questionnaire to retain the personal touch, though this is only recommended if your handwriting is very neat. Questionnaires do have an advantage over the personal interview in that the act of writing your responses to family questions, rather than answering them in the course of a 'chat', makes them feel more 'official'. For this reason, questionnaires often produce more reliable information. It's best to concentrate on one person at a time.

If, for example, you were writing to your great-aunt in New Zealand about your great-grandfather (her father), you could ask some or all of the following questions, depending on what you already knew:

- What was his name (including middle names) and did he have a nickname?
- Do you know where he was born and where he lived at different times in his life?
- What was the name of his wife? When and where did they marry? Did he marry more than once?
- Do you know when and where he died, and where he was buried (or cremated)?
- What was his occupation and where did he work?

- Was he in the army, navy, or did he take part in any wars? Do you have any medals of his?
- Was he a member of any church? Which schools or colleges did he go to?
- Do you have any letters or personal memorabilia?
- Do you have any photographs?
- Do you have copies of his birth, marriage and death certificates?

You could also send a copy of your tree in progress to give your great-aunt an overall picture of the family and to see where you fit in. If you can, try to send the questionnaire to two or three different people. Make sure the wording is exactly the same each time. This will enable you to get just about as close to a factually accurate account as it is possible to do without consulting official records. If information between the questionnaires does not tally, then you could go back to one relation and ask them if they are really sure about that particular date or detail. Just by introducing this slight doubt you may trigger a more accurate memory.

Hopefully, as they become more involved, your relations will become just as intrigued as you are by the research. A postal visit can be slightly impersonal, so make sure you let your relatives know how much you appreciate what they are doing for you. It can be quite time-consuming for all concerned, but if you manage to instil a feeling of a common goal then you can all get a lot out of the experience.

Photographs

Old photographs are a fascinating way of bringing genealogy to life. Until you have actually seen a picture of the ancestor you are interested in, then your research can feel somewhat mechanical and abstract.

Most families will have kept photographs and passed them down through the generations. Remember that it was only in the late nineteenth century that amateur photography became commonplace; prior to that, photography tended to be the preserve of the wealthy. Most people employed professional photographers to record special events such as weddings and baptisms. Such photographs are great news for the genealogist as they often feature several generations, plus cousins, aunts, uncles and friends, all in the same photograph.

Seeing a family resemblance across the different rows as they line up for the photograph is also fascinating.

Some of the people in the photographs will be neighbours or friends, rather than family members. This doesn't mean these people cannot be useful to you in your research. Your relation may well have been closer to their next-door neighbour than to their sister, for example. At best, a neighbour will quite likely be able to tell you more about your relation's everyday life, so if someone can give you enough information about a non-family member featured in a photograph then seek them out – they may be a rich source of information.

When you are visiting relatives yourself, why not take photographs of them and start building up your own family collection? Then you can place these beside the old photographs you have obtained to form a fascinating 'then and now' album.

The dating of photographs is a whole subject in itself and there are many publications that can help you with this (see Further Reading). If you're lucky, a family photograph will have a date on the back. If not, you may be able to date it fairly accurately from what you already know about the birth dates of the family members pictured. Otherwise, you need to consult with a specialist agency that will be able to date the photograph from the style of dress, hairstyles, hats, buildings and shops (if shown) and any writing (on shops signs, posters, etc.).

Genealogy vs social history

The discussion on photographs brings us to the wider subject of social history. Photographs from the time of your ancestors, such as street scenes, shipyard scenes, farming and other work-place based pictures, churches, festivals and fairs, and marketplace scenes can tell you a great deal about how your family lived. This is the realm of social history rather than genealogy, strictly speaking.

Social history and genealogy are generally regarded as distinct disciplines, but there is certainly a good deal of overlap. Social history encompasses all that genealogy is, plus a lot more. Personally I feel that taking a social historical approach to your research is more rewarding than simply concentrating on building up a diagrammatic tree, with birth, marriage and death dates. Photographs are often the springboard, as this is the point at which your ancestors become real people, who lived in a real town at a specific time. It's not only personal photographs of the family that are interesting. It can be just as rewarding to look at an old street scene and imagine your ancestor in the photograph, walking down *that* street, popping in to *that* tobacconist's and relaxing with a pint of bitter at *that* pub on the corner at the end of the day.

There are a large number of photographic libraries and specialist shops housing often huge collections of old photographs. The Hulton Getty archive (formerly the Hulton Archive) in West London is a phenomenal resource, holding some 40 million images. It owns the photographic archive of the journal *Picture Post* (published from 1937 to 1957), as well as a number of other historical collections. The library is constantly being added to. You can search the collection for free online (**www.hultonarchive.com**), or get an in-house researcher to research for you for a small fee.

Other comprehensive resources of early photographs are the National Monuments Record (which, as its name suggests, concentrates primarily on buildings), the

Imperial War Museum, The Royal Geographical Society Library and the National Maritime Museum, all of which are based in London.

Outside the capital are the Museum of English Rural Life in Reading and the Francis Frith Collection in Andover, which holds pictures of village life from over 2,000 British towns and villages. Popperfoto is another extensive library similar to the Hulton Archive, but on a smaller scale. You can do an online search for most of these libraries. At the time of writing, the National Monuments Record and National Maritime Museum do not have their collections online, but this could change very quickly. The Museum of English Rural Life, The Royal Geographical Society and the Imperial War Museum have samples of their collections online (these collections are huge and the process of scanning all material in order to make it available online is a massive task). The Hulton Archive, Francis Frith Collection and Popperfoto have far more extensive electronic libraries.

Real people, real lives

If you follow the guidelines set out above and prepare for your research in a sensible way then it will help you cope better with the frustrations that you will inevitably meet. The most important thing to remember is that family-tree research is not simply a technical exercise. It's about other people's lives, and your own. I've stressed in this chapter the importance of being sensitive to the feelings of relations. You also need to spare a thought for your own.

Genealogy can be incredibly frustrating. This is probably the emotion that you will experience most frequently when researching your tree. Frustration with not being able to find an entry in the official indexes, frustration when the respective stories of different relatives do not match up, and, worst of all, frustration with discovering that an entry you were absolutely certain was that of your relation turns out to be someone else altogether.

It can also be upsetting. While you're busy trying to deal diplomatically with information that you sense may upset other members of your family, don't forget that you may make troubling discoveries too. One of the most common reactions to making such a discovery is the feeling that your family have been hiding things from you, and this can lead to resentment. Visiting gravestones can also be tough.

Try to prepare yourself for this eventuality and think about why information may not have been passed on to you. Once you start to think about the motivation behind this, you'll realize that it was probably because your relatives believed it was best for you, or that you simply wouldn't be interested. If you find yourself harbouring feelings of resentment, try to talk

to your relations about it and explain how you feel. If this isn't working then don't push it. These discoveries and the feelings they give rise to are part and parcel of family-tree research. If you're serious about your research, then you must accept this.

And then there's the good news. The elation! Those 'Eureka' moments when you suddenly find a missing link that pulls your whole tree together and that makes all the frustrations worth it, when you suddenly realize why you started doing all this time-consuming research in the first place.

Finally, there are the unexpected personal rewards. The discovery of long-lost relations, who through the course of your research may become close friends, is a fantastic by-product of genealogy.

CHAPTER 3

SEARCHING THE OFFICIAL RECORDS

This chapter looks at the real nitty gritty of your family-tree research – using the records held at the Family Records Centre for England and Wales. Here we concentrate on the practicalities of researching the records, and some of the common stumbling blocks you may come up against, which should help you to be as well prepared as possible when you visit the centre.

The Family Records Centre

Since 1837, every birth, marriage and death in England and Wales has had by law to be recorded. This is known as Civil Registration. These records are held at the Family Records Centre (FRC), which is part of the General Register Office (GRO), run by the Office of National Statistics. Civil Registration is carried out by local civil registrars who report each birth, marriage or death to the Superintendent Registrar of the district, who sends copies of the records to the Registrar-General at the GRO every three months. This means that for each birth, marriage or death in England and Wales there are two certificates: one held by the Superintendent Registrar of the district in which the event took place and one held at the GRO.

For a long time housed in Somerset House on the Strand, the Family Records Centre has now moved to modern offices in Myddelton Street, Clerkenwell. The Centre is close to Angel tube (Northern line) and Farringdon tube and rail station (Circle and Metropolitan lines; Thameslink rail services). The office is signposted on major streets adjacent to Myddelton Street, such as Rosebery Avenue. The Family Records Centre occupies the ground floor of the building and the first-floor houses part of the Public Record Office (PRO), which contains important genealogical sources, including the Census (see Chapter 4).

A visit to the Family Records Centre is a pleasant experience. You might think that given the huge amount of information housed there it would be a slightly forbidding place, a maze of complex indexes and sources. The reality is quite the opposite. The centre is well-ordered and cleanly laid out. In fact it's hard to believe when you enter the new, almost minimalist main search room that every single birth, marriage and death since 1837 is actually recorded there. But it is. Surprisingly perhaps, the age range of the people visiting the records centre is about as broad as it could be. It would be a mistake to think of genealogy as a 'hobby for the elderly'. I saw people there perhaps as young as eighteen or nineteen scouring the indexes. The mix seemed about equal between the sexes.

For many people the Family Records Centre appears to be a sort of home from home. Many researchers seem to be on very friendly terms with other researchers and with the staff. They arrive when the centre opens in the morning (9.00 on Monday, Wednesday, Thursday and Friday, 9.30 on Saturday and 10.00 on Tuesday), put their belongings in the locker rooms in the basement (it's almost impossible to work with the indexes if burdened by more than just a pen and notebook), meet up with fellow researchers in the basement refreshment room for lunch and then go back to the indexes for the afternoon, probably until the centre closes (17.00 on Monday, Wednesday, Friday and Saturday, 19.00 on Tuesday and Thursday). And so on on the following day.

The website (**www.familyrecords.gov.uk**) offers probably the best introduction to the FRC and will help you prepare for your visit. The website explains what the centre contains and where each type of record is housed within the centre. If you don't have Internet access don't worry, the FRC is so clearly laid out that finding your way around will never be a problem.

New researchers sometimes go to the FRC hoping to come away with the actual birth certificate of their ancestor. This will not be possible, as the certificates themselves are held at the General Register Office based in Southport. The Family Records Centre simply holds the *indexes* to the certificates held by the GRO. Therefore you cannot obtain any certificate at the Family Records Centre itself. What you'll need to do is look up the entry in the indexes and give the GRO reference number (see page 53) to the staff, who will apply for the actual certificate by post. You can apply direct to the GRO in Southport yourself by e-mail, fax or post, but you'll have to give the index numbers from the FRC records anyway, so it's usually easiest to apply via the staff at the FRC.

The search begins

When you arrive at the Family Records Centre you'll be given some handouts on how to use the indexes.

However, it can be easier to ask one of the members of staff, most of whom are genealogy experts and are extremely helpful. Tell them it's your first time, explain what type of certificate you are looking for, from what period, and they will point you in the right direction.

The main area is organized into three separate sections: the indexes of births are red, marriages are green, and deaths are black. The indexes themselves are fairly hefty and just an hour or so's research can be quite telling on the arms, as you take down and replace volume after volume of these considerable tomes. In fact, the rhythm of the indexes being taken out and replaced provides a constant soundtrack to the centre, as researchers beaver away, sometimes at a quite frantic pace. The Family Records Centre is a relaxed and friendly place, and yet there is a certain urgency in the air. Maybe this is simply because people are often researching in their lunch hour, and their time is limited. But I think it's more because people get completely caught up in and mesmerized by what they are doing and increase the pace when they feel a goal might be within reach.

The indexes for births, marriages and deaths are organized under similar headings. I will concentrate first on births as these are what will be most relevant to you when researching your tree.

For most years there are four separate indexes. So births for 1899, for example, are organized into January to March (labelled Mar), April to June (labelled June), July to September (labelled Sept) and October to December (labelled Dec). For many periods the indexes are further sub-divided into letters (eg. Mar 1899 A–K, Mar 1899 J–O, Mar 1899 P–Z). The marriage and death indexes are organized in the same way.

A typical search

I knew that my grandmother, Mildred Dorothy Wycherley, was born in December 1899, because I remember from my childhood that she was 'as old as the year' (see her birth certificate on page 58). Therefore it was easy to find her entry, because I could go straight to the correct index (Dec 1899 P-Z). The fact that she had an unusual surname meant that once I got to the Wycherleys in the index there could be no doubt that I'd found the correct entry. There was in fact only one Mildred.

Finding the birth entry for her husband, Harry Ernest Screen, was more difficult (relatively speaking). My father had told me my grandfather's birth year, but I couldn't remember whether it was 1892 or 1893. I had no idea which month it was. I therefore had to search 7 volumes before I found his entry. Again, the unusual surname, Screen, meant that once I did get the right year and month it was easy to identify the correct entry. There were three other Screens but none shared my grandfather's Christian names, so, again, I could be confident I had found the correct entry.

A common surname

Well, bully for you, you might say. My name's Smith. Well, yes you do have a task ahead of you. But it's not an impossible one. You will find pages of Smiths, but gradually, by taking the information under each heading of the indexes, you will be able to eliminate them.

The birth index entries are organized under the following headings:

Surname   Initials   Place of birth   Volume   Page

Volume refers to the volume in which the actual certificate is held at the GRO in Southport, and **page** refers to the page of that particular volume. You will need to copy these reference numbers down carefully when applying for certificates.

Let's say you are looking for your great-grandfather, Arthur Smith, born in 1860. You can first rule out all the Smiths who are not called Arthur (from the four different volumes for 1860). If you know his middle initial this will be a great help and enable you to rule out many more, if not all, the other Smiths. If you do not know his initial, you may know his place of birth and this should help you whittle it down.

Of course it's perfectly possible that this will still leave you with more than one Smith to choose from – this happens all the time to people with a common surname, and occasionally to those with a far less common one. In this case you'll have to draw on any other information you have about Arthur Smith (either from birth certificates of his children or parents, or gleaned from visits or interviews with relatives) in order to move ahead with your research. You'll need to use the section on the back of the birth certificate application form, which is designed to help researchers who are not sure they have found the right entry in the indexes. Your answers to the questions on the back of the form, particularly point 5 (additional information), will help the GRO find the correct certificate. For example, you may know which field Arthur's father worked in – 'Father's Occupation' appears on the birth certificate.

Similarly, if you know Arthur's father's name, you can specify to the GRO that you wish only to receive the certificate that has this correct father's name (if you have made a mistake in your information and the certificate cannot be found you will receive a partial refund).

PLEASE REFER TO THE RED INDEX BOOKS TO COMPLETE THIS SECTION				
C 1837 - 1983	YEAR	QUARTER	DISTRICT	
1984 - 1992	YEAR	DISTRICT		REG
1993 ONWARDS	YEAR	DISTRICT Name and No.		

***Above** Close-up of section C of birth certificate application form shown on opposite page*

Searching the official records

Application for Full Birth Certificate CAS 51

USE THIS FORM ONLY TO ORDER CERTIFICATES
THROUGH THE PUBLIC SEARCH ROOM

PLEASE COMPLETE SECTIONS A-E IN BLOCK CAPITALS
BEFORE TAKING YOUR APPLICATION TO THE TILLS

A HOW MANY COPIES DO YOU REQUIRE ☐
(extra certificates are £6.50 each)

For purposes of detection and prevention of crime, information relating to this application may be passed on to other Government departments or law enforcement agencies

Entry No.

Taken out by

for office use only

TICK THE APPROPRIATE BOXES FOR QUESTIONS 1-3

1 ○ POSTED within 4 working days, first class post £6.50

2 ○ COLLECTION after 11am on the fourth working day £6.50 (on production of your receipt)

3 ○ 24 HOURS for a fee of £22.50 (COLLECTION)

4 Are you applying for your own certificate?

If not please state your relationship to the person whom the certificate relates

5 Explain your reasons for wanting a certificate

Please note that details supplied in section B will NOT be checked against the entry to which section C refers. If you are unsure you have found the correct entry see the back of this form

B Birth details

Surname at Birth	
Forenames	
Date of Birth	
Place of Birth	
Father's Surname	
Father's Forenames	
Mother's Maiden Surname	
Mother's Forenames	

E APPLICANT DETAILS

NAME

ADDRESS

SIGNATURE

TEL No   DATE

PLEASE REFER TO THE RED INDEX BOOKS TO COMPLETE THIS SECTION

C

| *1837 - 1983* | YEAR | QUARTER | DISTRICT | | VOL. | PAGE (Number following VOL) |

| *1984 - 1992* | YEAR | DISTRICT | | REG | VOL. | PAGE (Number following VOL) |

| *1993* ONWARDS | YEAR | DISTRICT Name and No. | | REG No. | ENT No. | DOR |

IMPORTANT
DO NOT FORGET TO REPEAT THE NAME
AND THE INDEX DETAILS BELOW
(SEE SECTIONS B+C)

D SURNAME AT BIRTH   FORENAMES

| *1837 - 1983* | YEAR | QUARTER | DISTRICT | | VOL. | PAGE (Number following VOL) |

| *1984 - 1992* | YEAR | DISTRICT | | REG | VOL. | PAGE (Number following VOL) |

| *1993* ONWARDS | YEAR | DISTRICT Name and No. | | REG No. | ENT No. | DOR |

Birth details

Surname at Birth	
Forenames	
Date of Birth	
Place of Birth	
Father's Surname	
Father's Forenames	
Mother's Maiden Surname	
Mother's Forenames	

Left Close-up of section B of birth certificate application form shown on page 55

ONLY USE THIS SIDE IF YOU ARE UNSURE THAT YOU HAVE THE CORRECT ENTRY

If, after completing the other side of this form, you are in doubt as to whether you have found the right entry, ask at the Customer Service Desk for leaflet CAS 62. Then, if you require reference(s) to be checked, fill in any space(s) below, where you are sure of the information.

A CERTIFICATE WILL BE PRODUCED ONLY IF THE PARTICULARS IN THE BIRTH RECORD AGREE PRECISELY WITH THOSE ENTERED BELOW. DETAILS WHICH DO NOT AGREE WITH THE ENTRY WILL BE CIRCLED. DETAILS NOT STATED ON AN ENTRY WILL BE MARKED 'N'S'. ONLY ENTER DETAILS BELOW IF YOU ARE CERTAIN OF THE INFORMATION.

1. Date of birth ....

2. Place of birth as exactly as possible ....

3. Full name and surname of person's father ....

4. Full name and maiden surname of person's mother ....

5. Other checking point ....

TO BE COMPLETED BY GENERAL REGISTER OFFICE:

CHECK POINT	REF 0	1	2	3	4	5	6	7	8	9	10
1											
2											
3											
4											
5											

Above Back of of birth certificate application form shown on page 55

You should fill in as much of the front of the form as you can from the information you have found in the index, and the other knowledge you have of your relation, in this case Arthur Smith. In section B of the form, Surname, Forenames and Place of Birth won't pose any problems, as this is exactly the information contained in the index entry. You may not be able to be absolutely precise as to the date of birth (remember that each index covers a 3-month period). Arthur's Father's Surname will normally be the same as his. Father's Forenames, Mother's Maiden Surname and Mother's Forenames you may not know, but searching the marriage indexes (see pages 60–61) should provide this information.

The birth certificate itself will take about three working days to arrive. You can collect it in person at the Family Records Centre or opt to have it posted to you.

Birth certificates have been modified slightly over the years, but the basic layout and headings remain the same. This is where your detective work can start, as the birth certificate contains information that will help you go back to the previous generation.

Left Close-up of columns 5, 6 and 7 of birth certificate pictured above

The birth certificate reproduced here is that of my grandmother, Mildred Dorothy Wycherley. It gives the surname and forenames of my grandmother's father, Harry Francis Wycherley, and the forename and maiden name of her mother, Caroline Law. The certificate also gives useful information about the father's occupation –

commercial traveller (tobacco), the name and address of the 'informant', in this case the father, and the district in which the birth was registered.

Starting to build a tree

From the information contained in my grandmother's birth certificate I can start to work backwards and build up a tree of that side of my family. I can hazard a pretty good guess at the birth year of my great-grandfather, Harry Francis Wycherley, from the information on this certificate. Say he was around 27 years old when he married, and perhaps had my grandmother a year later – that would make his birth year 1871. If this seems rather hit and miss, that's because it is. And that's why there is the constant hum of people pulling out and replacing indexes in the Family Records Office, as they pick on a year, fail to find the entry, and then work steadily through those years on either side of the one they have picked.

This is also where the extra bits of information you have obtained from your earlier visits to relatives really come into their own. For example, if I knew that Harry Francis Wycherley had a fairly long military career before marrying and starting a family then this would help in estimating his birth year. The column for Father's Occupation on the birth certificate may well give some pointers. If a relation has told you your great-grandparents married young, or if you have seen a dated wedding photograph of them, you may be able to take a stab at your great-grandfather's age at marriage and hence his birth date.

If you are unsure of a birth year, then you need to go via the marriage. A knowledge of general trends is incredibly useful in helping you establish a birth date – in 1871 professional men married at about 30, manual workers at about 24. In both cases women tended to be two years younger than the men. In general over the last two centuries, women have tended to be two years younger than men when they marry. Of course this is a generalization, but you've got to start somewhere and I've found awareness of such social trends to be incredibly useful when trying to find a route towards a birth entry.

I started by choosing a date that was one year before the birth of my grandmother (1898) for the marriage of Harry Francis Wycherley and Caroline Law. I was lucky to find the marriage entry in the indexes almost immediately. It won't always be so simple, and you should prepare yourself in particular for the discovery of illegitimacy. If the range of dates you have looked at yield nothing then it may be that the marriage took place after the birth of the first child, or did not take place at all.

From Harry Francis Wycherley's birth certificate I can then study the column for *his* father, estimate the marriage year of my great-great-grandparents and so on.

This marriage certificate is actually for my grandparents, not my great-grandparents, but from this you can still determine a relation's birth year. The certificate is dated

27 October 1928. Harry Ernest Screen was 36, so was born in either 1891 or 1892, most probably 1982. The marriage certificate therefore takes you with reasonable accuracy to the birth. You can then apply for the birth certificate in the normal way.

Your research will naturally become more difficult as you delve deeper into the past, as you will be drawing on less and less information from relatives and memorabilia you hold. In one specific way, however, it is easier: as you go back, population steadily decreases. The possibility of wrongly identifying an index entry as that of your relation therefore decreases (there is one rather than four indexes per year as you go back in time; the point at which this happens varies between births, marriages and deaths).

More about marriages

There are two main reasons why marriage certificates will be useful to you. First they give the wife's maiden name, so enabling you to research that line of the family, and second they give the age of both the bride and groom, so enabling you to determine their ages at birth and hence take you to their birth entries in the indexes. Marriage certificates are also very important for cross-checking names, dates and addresses with other certificates – you can never do too much cross-checking.

Searching the marriage indexes is considerably easier than searching the birth indexes. The main reason is that there are 50 per cent fewer marriages than births – it takes two to marry! Actually, the figure is lower than 50 per cent, as not everyone marries. The marriage entries are organized per individual and not per marriage. Therefore you will find an entry for your grandfather, and one for your grandmother somewhere else in the same volume of the indexes. The entries will be laid out as follows:

Screen　Harry E.　Wycherley　Atcham　6a　1377

And elsewhere in the index:

Wycherley　Mildred D.　Screen　Atcham　6a　1377

Obviously the volume and volume page numbers should match up. If they don't then one of the partners you have found is not your ancestor after all and you have no choice but to start again. It's best to look for the least common surname first and then find the matching entry. But even with the most common surnames the chances of finding more than one person are very slim – it would mean that all the variables in the column would have to match (i.e., middle initials, forenames, maiden names and district). In this sense marriage indexes are some of the most satisfying to search, particularly for common surnames.

Once you have found the marriage entry in the indexes, then you can apply for the actual marriage certificate. The application form is almost exactly the same as for the birth certificate, but less information is required in box B.

The certificate gives the names of both parties, including the woman's maiden name, their 'condition', profession, address, name, surname and profession of both fathers, and the signatures of witnesses. 'Condition' refers to whether they are a bachelor, spinster, widow, widower or divorced. A divorced man used to be described as 'the divorced husband of ...' (maiden name of previous wife). Now the wording is usually simply 'previous marriage dissolved'.

A divorced woman should remarry under the name by which she is known – this will be either her maiden name or her first married name. It's particularly important to watch out for this in family-tree research. If you are searching a female line and you take the maiden name as it appears on the marriage certificate as the route to her father, you will come up against a brick wall if the woman is actually using her first married name. If you find you are spending ages searching for a female ancestor in this way with no joy, then this is probably the reason. The best thing to do is to try to find the birth entry for a known brother or sister, which will give you the original maiden name you are looking for.

Another thing to bear in mind is that ages on marriage certificates are often given as 'full', which means 21 years of age or over. This was particularly common in Victorian times. Wives may have been 21 exactly, or several years older. Again, you may need to broaden your search of the birth indexes, as 21 may actually mean 25.

Since 1837, both the State and the Church have been able to conduct marriages in England and Wales. Between 1754 and 1837, only Church of England marriages were valid. At both church and civil ceremonies the bride and groom sign the register after the ceremony. At a Church of England wedding a certificate is kept by the married couple, one copy of the register is kept by the Church, and one is sent to the Superintendent Registrar of the region once it is full of names. The church minister must also send copies of entries to the GRO every three months.

Non-conformist (Jewish, Quaker, Roman Catholic, etc.) marriages take place either as a civil ceremony conducted by a local registrar in a civil registry office or are conducted by a civil registrar in a building used for Roman Catholic or non-conformist worship. As with church ceremonies, registers must be sent to the Superintendent Registrar and GRO. The registration procedure can also be carried out by an 'Authorized Person' – usually the priest or a member of the congregation – when a Registrar is not present. The Authorized Person then has the responsibility of sending quarterly registers to the Superintendent Registrar.

Death certificates

These are not as useful to the genealogist as birth and marriage certificates, but you should not make the mistake of ignoring them; they can be a particularly helpful cross-checking resource. In fact, death generates a large amount of records – doctor's certificate, hospital record, coroner's report, undertaker's bills, grave register entry, the grave itself, order for cremation, cremation record, burial or funeral service entry, and a will. As such it can sometimes provide the missing information you need. The details on a death certificate are as follows:

• Name of deceased

• Date and place of death

• Cause of death

• Age or date of birth of the deceased

• Deceased's occupation

• Signature, name and address of informant.

Deaths were often not registered in the places they occurred, so the place of death information is not always the most useful. However, the address will show where the relative was living at the time of death and this information can help you locate the family in the census (see Chapter 4). The informant may be a doctor or neighbour, and in such cases the information on age is unreliable. More often than not, however, the informant is a close relative – spouse, son or daughter. The age and hence the date of birth of the deceased can therefore be presumed to be accurate.

If you have struggled to find an ancestor's birth certificate, their death certificate is a good alternative source as it gives either age or date of birth. Death certificates also have an advantage over birth certificates in that from 1837 registration was virtually 100 per cent, since burial was only permitted on production of a death certificate. Furthermore, deaths had to be registered within five days of the event, so age on a death certificate (and hence date of birth) is very reliable.

A word on wills

If you cannot locate a death certificate, then you may be able to find a will, which in any case can tell you more about the deceased than a death certificate. A will gives the date of death, where the deceased was living at the time (which can help locate their family in the Census), who the will's worldly goods were going to (the executor/s) and the relationship between this individual or individuals and the deceased, the value of the deceased's goods and the date and location of probate (when and where the will was proved). It also gives the deceased's signature, which can be useful for cross-checking.

In 1858, the responsibility for proving wills passed from the Church of England to the State. Wills are proved in any one of the district probate offices in England and Wales (it does not have to be the probate office for the district in which the deceased died or lived). The national index to these wills, together with the wills themselves, is held at First Avenue House, 42–49 High Holborn, London WC1V 6NP. Copies of the index are also available on microfiche at the Family Records Centre.

If a will was not made, or for some reason invalid (the executors renounced their rights, for example) you may find a Letter of Administration. These are issued by the local probate court and give the next of kin the right to administer the estate. They provide the date and occupation of the deceased but do not have the amount of detail of wills. These are also held at First Avenue House.

Prior to 1858 the Church of England was responsible for proving wills (through the archdeacon of the particular district). These can be more difficult to find – your first port of call should be local records offices, which will have indexes of wills listed by date of probate and arranged alphabetically by surname. There is no national index to these records. The PRO also holds the records of the Prerogative Court of Canterbury, which covered pre-1858 wills for most of the southern half of the country. Records for Yorkshire and Nottinghamshire are held by the Borthwick Institute in York.

Before the nineteenth century, it was common for testators to list their grandchildren as well as all their children on the will, so a will can enable you to chart three generations of your tree (as always, you should check the information against any other sources you have). There may be several entries with the same name as your ancestor in the index. You need to draw on all the information you have in order to eliminate as many of these as possible, but it's a good idea to look at the wills of other people with the same name just to be sure. It's here that signatures can be crucial. If you have a marriage certificate for your ancestor, for example, you should be able to compare the signature on this and on the will.

Along with the usual reasons of illegibility, inconsistent spelling, poor indexing and your own human error when searching the indexes, you may also fail to find an entry because the will was proved late, or because of a 'second probate' (the original executor having died). It's therefore important to look at indexes for two or even three years after the date of death. Perhaps the most important thing to remember when searching for wills is that many people simply did not make one. If you have researched as thoroughly as you possibly can and still cannot find your ancestor's will, then you may have to accept that this was the case.

Tying it all together

So, by using a combination of birth, marriage and death entries, you can start to work steadily through the records and form your tree. Once you have worked back through one generation of birth certificates you can repeat the process. Study your great-grandfather's birth certificate. Look for the name of his father. Make an educated guess at the date of his marriage (say a year or two before the birth), look for the marriage entry in the indexes, and from this calculate his birth year. Easy. If only it were that simple.

Stumbling blocks

In an archive of around 270 million entries, which is what the Family Records Centre is, human error can never be eliminated. If you are having problems finding an index entry and are puzzled as to why, then use the following as a checklist. (These are worded to apply to births. Many of the stumbling blocks will be the same for marriages and deaths too. Where there is a problem particular to marriages or deaths, I have mentioned it separately.)

Your eye has missed the entry. It's the obvious one. You may well be searching through a list that has pages and pages of the same surname. You may have been doing it for several hours and your eyes may be very tired. Go down to the refreshment room for a coffee then return to the index and look again. I bet it's there.

There is confusion over the indexes. As we have seen, the indexes for one year are usually divided into quarterly periods. You will probably be working alongside other researchers who are using the same volumes. With all this taking down and replacing of indexes it can be difficult to remember which ones you have looked at. It's worth noting down as you go the month and year of each index you have searched so as not to lose your place.

Misreading of the certificate. Look at the close-up of columns 6, 7 and 8 of my grandparents' marriage certificate on the following page (see page 61 for the full certificate). The handwriting is almost illegible. Unless you know the town, then the addresses are incredibly difficult to decipher (they are 11 Falstaff Street, Shrewsbury and Armoury Terrace, Shrewsbury), as are the Fathers' Occupations (coach builder and insurance agent). Although this particular information wouldn't be needed for the index entry, it certainly illustrates how errors can creep in.

Residence at the time of Marriage.	Father's Name and Surname.	Rank or Profession of Father.
11 *Falstaff Street* Shrewsbury	Henry Robert Severn	Coach builder
Asbury Terrace Shrewsbury	Harry Harris Wyckley	turnway agent

Close-up of columns 6, 7 and 8 of marriage certificate

The birth was not registered. Although registration became compulsory in 1837, many people were not aware of the new law, or believed that baptism served the same purpose and it was not necessary to have a child both baptized and registered. It has been estimated that around 10 per cent of all births between 1837 and 1875 were not registered. If this is the case, then baptismal records (see Chapter 6) may well provide the information you are looking for.

Similarly, the marriage may not have been registered. If you cannot find the marriage entry, consider the possibility that your relations lived as a married couple but never actually went through the ceremony. They may even have been known as 'Mr and Mrs', but officially were not.

If a death has not been registered, this could be because the body could not be identified.

Birth and registration dates do not match. If you know the birth date of your ancestor but the only possible match for him or her is dated over a month later, then do not assume this cannot be your ancestor. Legal registration could take place up to 42 days after the birth. From 1875 fines were imposed for late registration. There's no doubt that people would frequently lie to avoid payment of the penalty and claim a child was born in October, when in fact the birth was in July. You should bear this in mind if you are having problems finding a birth entry, and increase the scope of your search to include more indexes to either side of your starting point.

The birth was registered in another area. You know where your ancestor lived, but cannot find the entry. It's possible the family moved just before or just after the birth. In Victorian times there was far more geographical mobility than you might think, and this increased at key moments such as marriage and after the birth of the first child. It might help to find the index entries of siblings, therefore.

The birth was registered outside England and Wales, perhaps at sea. This was particularly common during times of colonial expansion. There was no legal obligation to register an overseas birth with the authorities in England and Wales and many did not bother. There are a number of sources held by the GRO that can help you if you feel this might be why you cannot find an entry. These include a register of births and deaths at sea from 1837, another of births and deaths in the air dating from 1948 and one for births and deaths on hovercraft(!) dating from 1972. Records of soldiers missing in action are held by the War Office at the PRO.

The child was adopted. Searching for the records of an adopted child is difficult and you should be realistic about this as you are unlikely to be able to take your tree research very far if you know that your ancestor was adopted. Adoption did not become legal until 1927 and it's almost impossible to find records prior to that date. Certificates of legal adoptions are held at the Family

Records Centre. The adopted child will probably have been brought up using the name of the adoptive parents, whereas the name on the birth certificate is most likely to be that of the natural mother. The records of organizations such as Barnados could be a useful source.

The child was illegitimate. Over the last 150 years about 5 per cent of all births have been illegitimate. The illegitimate child will usually be registered under the mother's maiden name. From 1875 onwards, if the father was known he could be named on the certificate, but only if he were: a) consenting; b) present at the registration. Understandably, the certificates for most illegitimate children have a blank in the box for the father's name. If the mother later marries, and the child is known by the surname of the new husband, it can be very difficult to find their birth entry, which will be under the mother's maiden name.

Change of name. It's possible that you cannot find an entry because your ancestor changed their name. There is no legal impediment to changing your name – you or I could do it tomorrow. The law cites 'usage' as the only criteria. If the new name is being used, then that is your legal name. Generally, however, people like to change their name by deed poll, which is by way of application to the Supreme Court. The name given to a child at birth can be legally changed up to twelve months after the initial registration. A new certificate is then issued. Few people are aware of this rule and it's actually very rare for a name to be changed in this way.

An awareness of the above pitfalls will put you in a very good position when studying the civil registration records and should help you avoid some of the common mistakes of beginner family-tree researchers.

CHAPTER 4

THE CENSUS

Census records are important to the family-tree researcher both as an alternative to birth, marriage and death certificates, and as a complement to them. They are great for cross-checking information found on civil registration certificates, but they also provide interesting additional information. The census manuscripts are held in the form of microfilm or microfiche by the Public Record Office (PRO) on the first floor of 1 Myddelton Street. As with the Family Records Centre, there is no charge for viewing and you can buy copies of microfilms for a small fee.

The census takes place every ten years in England and Wales and the first one took place in 1801. This means that the census records can take you back a little further than the civil registration records, which date from 1837. The other main difference is that census records are not organized by name but by district, and by street within those districts. Therefore you will need to know the address (or at least the district) of your ancestors in order to find them in the census records.

Census records are only made available to the public 100 years after the census is taken, for reasons of confidentiality. The 1901 Census is now available (see Recent Census Developments, page 96). It's not impossible to view records from the last 100 years, but you will have to write to the Registrar General with a good reason for your being granted this access. You will pay a fairly hefty fee for the privilege too. This information is only available to direct descendants.

Censuses have traditionally taken place on a Sunday night. Historically there has been much disagreement over this, as many have argued that this is not at all a good time for the census, since people tend to go away for the weekend. For a time the day was changed to Monday, but then reverted to Sunday.

The officials who carried out the census were known as 'enumerators', with the map of England and Wales divided into over 600 enumeration districts. Enumerators would distribute the census form to the head of the household, or the head of the organization in the case of workhouses, prisons, boarding schools etc., for completion. In the case of illiteracy, the enumerator would fill in the form for the head of the household, based on his or her verbal responses to the questions.

The type of information recorded by the census has changed over time. Between 1801 and 1831 the census was very basic and amounted to little more than a head count. Records from this period show the number, sex and age of the people in a household, but not their names. Therefore, they are not of great use to the genealogist. In any case, most of these returns were subsequently destroyed. A few enumerators did list the names of householders (guidelines were not strict) and limited numbers of these lists survive in parish records.

From 1841 the census started to become more sophisticated and the questions more comprehensive. By 1851, age and place of birth of each person were included and, critically for the genealogist, the relationship to the head of the household. If you are using the 1841 Census, before the relationship to the head of the household was included, you should be wary of making assumptions about relationships. Ages were often rounded down to the nearest five years. This can mean that two individuals can appear to be father and daughter when in fact they are husband and wife (a young wife of nineteen, rounded down to fifteen, and a husband of 35, for example).

The PRO Census Reading Room

The census reading room at 1 Myddelton Street is an impressive place. As with the Family Records Centre, you are struck by the contrast between this modern space and the vast amount of ancient manuscript it houses.

The first area of the reading room you will come to contains the street indexes, the surname indexes and registration district indexes. You need these in order to find the right piece of microfilm of the particular census you are interested in. There are also two very useful maps that show how England and Wales was divided up into its respective registration districts. One map covers the period 1837–51, the other 1852–1946.

The census records are arranged on microfilm in the form of 'pieces'. A piece simply means a part of the film. A piece can cover a number of enumeration districts, or, if a district was particularly large, it can take up more than one piece. There are detailed instructions at various points in the census room to guide you through the process of finding your way through the indexes, and hence finding the right place on the film.

A sample search

When I wanted to look for the family of my great-grandfather, Henry Robert Screen, in the census, I did not at that time have their street address. Staff at the PRO will tell you that you are up against it if you don't know the street in which your ancestors lived, but given that I had the name of their village, I thought it was worth a shot. If your ancestors lived in a large city and you do not know the name of the street, then you will definitely have problems and you need first to try to find the street name from another source, such as letters, postcards, directories, the electoral roll, rate books, etc.

From the marriage indexes for Henry Robert Screen and Mary Ann Ellis, I knew that they got married on 25 December 1884 at Winterbourne Clenstone, England. Now, Winterbourne Clenstone sounded like a pretty small village to me, which, as I said, made me feel I had a good chance of finding them on the census without knowing the street name. My starting point was therefore the census of 1891 (I was hoping that in the intervening seven years Henry and Mary had not moved house).

The Census

In the census room I proceeded as follows:

1. I looked up Winterbourne Clenstone in the Place Name Index and found it was a sub-district of the registration district Blandford.

2. I noted down the registration district number of Blandford – 260.

3. I turned to the Registration District Indexes and found 260 (these numbers are highlighted in yellow throughout the index). This then gave me a class code and a piece number for the film.

4. I noted down the class code (RG12) and the piece number (1633). Now I could proceed to find the film. I took a 'black box' and went to the film cabinets to find the film that covered RG12/1633, which was RG12/1632–1634. The black box is simply a pass in the same size and shape as the boxes of microfilm with a seat number on it, and provides a way of monitoring who is working with which film. When you find the correct film in the cabinet you physically substitute this film with your black box, so that when someone is looking for the same piece of film they can find you at your seat, at your film reader. The reading area has about 300 seats.

5. I took the film to my allotted microfilm reader and loaded the film – there are handouts at the end of each row of readers explaining how to do this.

6. I wound the film on until I got to section 1633. In that section were just a few enumeration districts, one of which was Winterbourne Clenstone. (If I'd know the street, I would also have been able to find a folio and page number, taking me to the exact place on the film).

7. You can spot the start of a new enumeration district quite easily when winding through the film as each starts with a statement from the enumerator and a summary of the streets covered.

8. I did not find Henry Robert and Mary Ann Screen.

They had moved.

This, unfortunately, is often the experience of researchers using the census and arises from the fact that the original source of the address or village (most probably the birth certificate) is highly unlikely to have the same date as the census – in my experience there was a difference of seven years between the original source (in this case a marriage index) and the census. In fact, it was hardly surprising the family had moved.

At this point, I realized that it would have been much better to search for the birth date of one of the children, born closer to the date of the census. Henry Robert and Mary Ann's son, Harry Ernest, was born in January 1892, in Atcham, Shropshire. The 1891 Census took place in April 1891, just 9 months before Harry's birth. It was therefore highly likely that Atcham is where they would have been living. I went through the whole process again. Atcham was indeed where they were living at the time of the 1891 Census.

It's easy to see how census research can be trying on your patience. Even the process of winding the microfilm to the appropriate place can take a considerable amount of time. Staff at the PRO tend to meet statements such as 'I don't know where they lived but it was somewhere in Liverpool' with a look that betrays both pity and world-weariness in equal amounts. The process sounds complex, but really it's pretty straightforward once you get there, and there are always other eager researchers willing to show you the ropes.

If, like me in the above example, you do not have a street address and therefore cannot use the street indexes, then a surname index is about your only realistic hope of finding the family on the census. If you know your family lived in a small parish of less than 4,000 people then you can quite easily search the microfilm for this number of entries in less than an hour, so it's no real handicap to not have a surname index. However, for larger towns and cities the surname index is indispensable.

The compilation of surname indexes is an ongoing process. The surname index for the 1881 Census is now complete, and the 1851 index is almost complete. This work is generally undertaken by family history societies (see Chapter 5) or by (extremely) dedicated individuals. It is a huge task. For other census years particular counties have been indexed, others have not. If you refer to the Place Name Index at the PRO, you will see a note next to the place name telling you whether a surname index exists for that particular place.

Using the 1881 Census index

An incredible amount of electronic indexing work has been done for the 1881 Census – not only has it been indexed by surname, but also by birthplace and census place. In the birthplace index individuals are listed in alphabetical order of surname and then (within each surname) the names are sorted by birthplace. In the census place index individuals are listed in alphabetical order of surname and then (within each surname) by where they lived at the time of the census.

I used the surname index to search for my great-grandfather Henry Robert Screen in the 1881 Census. I knew he was born in December 1856, so would have been 24 at the time of the April 1881 Census. The index search asks you to key in surname, forename, age or date of birth, and census place (by county and district). However, with a fairly unusual surname simply keying in the surname and forename will be enough – you won't be overwhelmed with matches.

From this search I retrieved a screen showing the four members of the Screen family living in the same household as Henry Robert at the time of the 1881 Census. The screen gives the class code, piece number, folio and page, so you can go straight to collect the correct film and take it to be photocopied. You don't even have to view the film on the microfilm reader, but it's a good idea to, just to reassure yourself that your family is actually where the index says it is.

The relevant page of film for my family showed the four Screens: Robert (Henry's father), Elizabeth (Henry's mother), Julia (Henry's sister) and Henry.

Columns 1 and 2 gave the name and number of the street, column 3 the person's name, column 4 the relationship to the head of household, column 5 the condition (married, widower, etc), column 6 the age last birthday (split into two sub-columns for men and women), column 7 the occupation, and column 8 the place of birth. My search showed a fairly typical example of the difficulty of deciphering an enumerator's hand. The enumerator's oblique slashes next to the names mark the end of one household and the start of the next. Unfortunately they sometimes also obscure the writing.

When I looked at the occupation column, Henry and Julia's occupations, Coach Builder and Dress Maker respectively, were not too difficult to make out. But their father Robert's occupation, Soap Boiler, was less clear. It took me a few attempts to work this one out – I was only confident I had read it correctly by comparing other occurrences of certain letters, particularly this enumerator's rather elaborate 'p'.

General research problems

Censuses are fascinating documents, and the information contained in them can really bring your research to life, as you imagine all the different members of the household congregating as the head of the household fills out the forms on census night. The information is often incomplete, however, and can be inaccurate. These are the main reasons:

Family member not present. The census recorded only those present in the household on the specific day of the census, at the specific time of the enumerator's visit. There are many different reasons why a family member may have been absent. They could have been away on business, serving in the army or navy, in an institution such as prison, hospital or a boarding house, or working as a domestic servant or farm labourer (on the night of the 1861 Census, 24,000 people were recorded as being in prison).

Or they could just have been out for the night – on a date or in the alehouse – although this was not common, as the households knew when the census was to take place and few families deliberately avoided it.

The family had moved. If you are taking information from a birth certificate, say, and using this to locate an entry in the census, you may encounter problems. For example, you have the birth certificate of your grandmother, born in 1855, and want to find the family's entry in the census. You cannot assume that by the 1861 Census the family will be in the same place as that recorded on the birth certificate. You will have to establish their whereabouts from another record, perhaps the birth certificate of a younger sibling.

Handwriting. You only need to remember my difficulty in reading the 1881 Census entry to see what a major stumbling block handwriting can be. The legibility of an enumerator's hand varied enormously. Some wrote neatly within the columns, others veered off into the margins.

Slapdash enumerators often left out the number of the house and just entered the street name. Deciphering the enumerator's hand can be part of the fun, and rewarding when you crack it, but there's no doubt it adds to the unreliability of the records.

Illegibility partly due to the transfer of the manuscript census forms to the microfilm. The 1861 Census is notorious in this respect.

Illiteracy. With an illiterate family, or a where the head of the household could not complete the forms for some other reason, the enumerator wrote down information based on the verbal responses to his questions. This could lead to inaccuracies if the enumerator: a) misheard; b) spelt a name wrongly; c) omitted any information.

Individuals missed. Sometimes people were simply missed by the enumerator. Children were sometimes hidden away as the family didn't want to face accusations of overcrowding.

Dates unreliable. The enumerator had to rely on the information given by the head of the household. Ages can often be wrong – not because the head of household was lying, but because he simply didn't know, or had forgotten, the ages of all the members of his household. Often ages are rounded down. This was particularly common when an extended family, including aunts, uncles and in-laws, were living under one roof. Women often lied about their age, particularly if they had a younger husband. Children's ages could be massaged upwards for employment purposes. Comparing consecutive censuses where the family has stayed in the same home can reveal how inaccurate ages can be.

Street 'breaks off'. A particular street does not always appear in one unbroken list. The normal practice for the enumerator was to start on one side of the street, then as soon as a side street was reached list the households on both sides of the side street, return to the main street until the second side street was reached, etc. Streets can therefore be broken up quite extensively in the census. Another problem to watch out for is a particularly long street that is in more than one registration district, so it appears in two separate places on the census.

As I have said, you can't search the census records without knowing the district in which your ancestors lived at the time of the census. If the birth, marriage or death certificates cannot help you in this respect, you could try any of the following:

Electoral rolls. These sometimes hold information that is missing from the censuses. Electoral rolls from 1832 are held at Town Halls and Local Records Offices. Remember that women did not appear on the electoral roll until 1927.

Trade directories. The most useful is probably Kelly's, which listed householders, often to help travelling salesmen. Others are army lists, medical registers, shipping registers and a whole host of specialist professional directories, many of which are available at the PRO in Kew (see Chapter 5).

Rate books. Local authority rate books (from the nineteenth century onwards) have details of the properties upon which rates were imposed, so can help in finding addresses. You should apply to local parishes for copies.

Specific employers. Long-established organizations such as the Post Office and the Police often hold considerable information about former employees.

Recent census developments

In January 2002, the 1901 Census became available online. This is an exciting project and marks the first time a complete census has been available on the Internet. It is hoped that the 1891 Census will also be completely digitalized by the end of 2002, and feasibility studies into the possibility of making all existing censuses available online is underway. For the 1901 Census online, a pilot programme was carried out for Norfolk and from the feedback from this the PRO established the best way of setting up the complete site, the most effective ways to search and how to organize the records. You can get news of it at **www.census.pro.gov.uk**.

Census research is both hugely rewarding and hugely frustrating. Reading the enumerator's books, written in their original hand, on microfilm can certainly transport you back in time and there's an undeniable adrenalin rush when you see the names of your ancestors on the often battered manuscript pages. The ongoing process of indexing is key to facilitating census research and there has been huge progress in this area over recent decades, particularly with surname indexes.

Researching outside London

So far I have concentrated on the genealogical records held at the Family Records Centre and Census Reading Room of the PRO. You could be forgiven for thinking that family-tree research only ever takes place in London. Fortunately, this is far from the case. There are a number of alternative sources of genealogical information, the main ones being local records offices, the Society of Genealogists, family history societies and one-name societies. As we will see in Chapter 7, the Internet means that national as well as regional barriers to research are increasingly being removed.

Local Records Offices

Most counties have at least one local records office, some have several. These may be housed in the public library or in a separate local authority building. They contain a wealth of information of interest to the genealogist and provide a more manageable alternative to London. Local records offices usually buy in microfilm copies of the parts of the census that cover their area and these can be consulted in the same way as at the PRO. Remember that many former counties are now metropolitan districts (e.g., London Metropolitan Archives). Local Records Offices may also hold any of the following for their particular area:

- Civil registration records
- Parish registers, bishop's transcripts and marriage licence records (see Chapter 6)
- CD-Rom copies of the International Genealogical Index (see below)
- Publications of local historians and local family history societies
- Trade directories
- Local education and court records
- Rate books
- Electoral rolls
- Military and naval registers
- Wills
- Photographs and maps.

Where the amount of records is considerable, and it often is, local records offices have produced indexes and guides to help you in your search – not all are organized in the same way. Generally any search is free of charge. It's a good idea to phone first to check on opening times and availability of indexes so that you can be as well prepared as possible before you go.

As well as county and metropolitan archives there are a number of local history museums in England and Wales that will also be of use and may hold additional material. You can find these in *Yellow Pages* or the phone book, or through a family history society.

The Society of Genealogists

The archive of the Society of Genealogists (SoG) is a phenomenal resource, and the library has the most comprehensive source of family-tree information in the whole of Britain. The SoG is a charity whose mission is to 'promote, encourage and foster the study, science and knowledge of genealogy'. It is London-based (14 Charterhouse Buildings, Goswell Road, London EC1M 7BA), but the records it holds can also be found in many family history societies, local records offices and on the

Internet. It has its own publication programme and organizes many talks, lectures and short courses. Its bookshop is considerably larger than that at the Family Records Centre. You may wish to become a member of the SoG and receive a quarterly journal, together with news of and discounts on events and publications.

The SoG holds similar resources to the local records offices, but for the whole of England and Wales rather than for local areas: microfilm copies of the census and of the indexes of births, marriages and deaths; parish registers (the widest collection in the country, with over 9,000 registers); non-conformist registers; directories; and many other more specialist records.

It also holds some international records, such as births, marriages and deaths in parts of the US, Australia and a number of other Commonwealth countries, and the complete civil registration indexes for Scotland, and as such may supplement your research at the Family Records Centre. The SoG also holds the International Genealogical Index (IGI) for the whole world on microfiche and the database FamilySearch on CD-Rom, which includes the IGI (see below).

Mormon Family History Centres and the IGI

Yes, those ever-so-polite young men with their gleaming white teeth have made a huge contribution to international genealogy. The Mormons, or to give them their official name, The Church of Jesus Christ of Latter Day Saints (LDS) have made every researcher's task a lot easier by creating the International Genealogical Index (IGI).

The reason the Mormons are so dedicated to family history research is that they believe they can posthumously baptize their ancestors into the Mormon faith, and therefore they seek to build up a tree of as many ancestors as they possibly can.

The IGI is the world's most important finding aid for records pre-dating civil registration in 1837. The LDS library in Salt Lake City, Utah, is the world's largest genealogical library. The obvious advantage of it over other records is that it holds records *for the whole world*. As I said in the Introduction, this is not the book for you if you know that your ancestors came from outside England and Wales, but the IGI will be a starting point.

Fortunately, you won't need to make a trip to Salt Lake City to consult the IGI. The Mormons operate about 60 family history centres in England and Wales, and each one holds microfilm and CD-Rom copies of the IGI. The LDS library in Salt Lake City also holds vast amounts of other microfilmed material, such as parish registers, census records and wills. You will need to order these films, but this is straightforward as the family history societies all hold indexes to the material, from which you can find the film number.

The Mormons have produced a database called FamilySearch, which holds both the IGI and a program called Ancestral File, which is a collection of information submitted by LDS members about their ancestors. Ancestral File is good fun because by using certain options it allows you to create mini pedigrees and descendancy charts, so creating a family tree diagram on screen. The information contained in Ancestral File, however, is far from complete for the whole world, so you shouldn't assume that the tree it creates for you has all the rights dates and spellings, or even the right people.

When I used the IGI to create a descendancy chart for my great-grandfather Henry Robert Screen, I found that my *grandfather* was also listed as Henry Screen, when in fact his name was Harry Screen (this was his baptized name, not a nickname for Henry). The date of a marriage was also incorrect. The IGI is thus never a substitute for searching the original records.

Family History Societies

Not to be confused with the Mormon's family history centres, these are local groups that are set up and run independently by individuals and local historians, often closely linked to but separate from local records offices.

If you are a beginner in genealogy then joining a Family History Society (FHS) is highly recommended. Local records offices can provide a list of FHS operating in your area. Family History Societies make an important contribution to ongoing research into the genealogy of local areas and most publish magazines in which members provide information about their ancestors. There is also much fruitful exchange between Family

History Societies in different parts of the country. The Federation of Family History Societies (FFHS) is the umbrella organization of which all the individual societies are members.

Your local FHS might not in fact be the most useful one for you to join. If you know that your ancestors lived in a particular area for a few generations, then you should consider joining the FHS for that area. One of the first things you might discover is that another society member is already researching the same family. This is the advantage of operating at a local level. Many genealogists actually join both their local FHS and others that are based in areas where their ancestors lived. This means they have the practical advantage of a local FHS, while still maximizing the resources of other societies.

One of the most appealing aspects of the FHS is the sense of community and shared interests that it provides. Genealogy can at times feel like a rather solitary pursuit. If you limit your research to the Family Records Centre and the Internet you may well find all the information you are looking for, but you are really missing out on the social aspect of genealogy. Family-tree research can yield some exciting discoveries. I witnessed a woman punch the air with glee while sitting at a microfilm reader at the PRO. She clearly wanted to share her joy, but realized that in a large room full of complete strangers it was probably best to keep it to herself. No doubt she later went to her local FHS meeting and was able to tell of her discovery.

Family history societies contribute probably more than any other body to the advancement of research at a local level. They have made an enormous contribution to indexing records and registers across the country. Somerset and Dorset Family History Society, for example, has transcribed the details of all the marriages from the register books of Dorset parishes from 1538 to 1837 (the start of civil registration). The index is virtually complete. Many other FHS volunteer members dedicate an enormous amount of time to meticulously transcribing and indexing entries from parish registers, for the benefit of current and future genealogists.

One-name societies

These are of particular interest if you have an unusual surname. Many thousands of family names are being researched by individuals or groups, their aim being to record every single occurrence of that name worldwide. A good starting point if you want to find out whether your name is subject to an ongoing study is GOONS – the Guild of One-Name Studies. Write to the Registrar of the Guild care of the SoG's address, or contact them via their website (see Chapter 7).

Many one-name researchers start with a local area they know to be rich in occurrences of that name, then gradually broaden their search. To research a name internationally is not for the fainthearted (and the Guild only accepts members who are researching internationally) and you must be prepared for a long haul. If you can't find any evidence that the name you wish to work on is currently being researched then go for it, but make sure you think carefully about the time it will involve. One-name researchers tend to see themselves as a rather special breed, operating in the rarefied atmosphere of the higher echelons of genealogy.

The Guild's members' activities should help spur you on – they organize many lectures and produce publications, including *The Journal of One-Name Studies*, published quarterly.

You may be one of the thousands of people who at some point have received letters from an organization called Halberts offering you a book that lists all the people sharing your name in the world, in exchange for the payment of a fee. I have one such book of Screens. Often these are simply compiled from telephone directories and are of little real value to the genealogist. The information may be of some interest in that it can reveal geographical concentrations of your name, but beyond that it tells you very little as there are so many omissions. You have been warned.

The PRO

We have already come across the Public Record Office (PRO) in the shape of the Census Reading Room, located on the first-floor of 1 Myddelton Street in London. The remainder of the PRO archives are housed at Kew (Ruskin Ave, Kew, Richmond, Surrey TW9 4DU). The PRO, traditionally the repository of all national archives, is a vast resource and I'm not going to go into what it holds in great detail here. One of the great advantages that the PRO has over other records centres is that the type of information it holds is more specialist. This is the case particularly for military and naval records.

To tackle the PRO records you'll find that you need plenty of help from indexes and information leaflets. There are over a hundred 'Records Information Leaflets' that refer to different areas of the archive. To give you an idea of the extent of the archive, the *Current Guide* to using the PRO runs to 5,500 pages, and that's just a usage guide, before you've even started researching the records themselves.

Don't despair though, you will probably be searching for something very specific and you can find the relevant records fairly easily using the Records Information Leaflets. Perhaps the best way to use the PRO's resources is as a supplement to the Family Records Centre. For example, if you are looking for birth dates you have not been able to find at the FRC, and you know that one or more generations of your family were employed by the Royal Marines, then the PRO is the place for you. The PRO holds the archives of the War Office, the Admiralty and the Home Office.

Other specialist records include:

- Army, navy, airforce and merchant navy records
- Non-conformist and non-parochial registers of baptisms, marriage and burials (see Chapter 6)
- Taxation records
- Property records
- Wills, administrations and death duties
- Railway records

Within these, you can find an incredible amount of detail. For example, naval records may contain captain's log books, accounts, correspondence, journals, etc.

Research at the PRO is carried out by a 'class' and 'piece' method similar to that in operation at the Census Reading Room. All sections of documents have a reference number composed of letters and numbers such as WO 27 (War Office 27). Within a section a particular piece number will contain more specialist records, for example, piece 1795 of WO 27 could contain records of a particular regiment.

As with the FRC, access to the PRO records is free of charge and copies can be provided for a small charge. On the ground floor are a restaurant, cloakroom and bookshop, which is a good job, as you'll probably be in for a long stay!

CHAPTER 5

DELVING DEEPER

So far we have concentrated on looking at records from the early 1800s onwards. Now it's time to go further back in history by looking at the parish church registers of baptisms, marriages and burials.

You might presume that the further back you go, the more difficult your research becomes. This is not necessarily the case, as some parish registers are virtually complete and perfectly preserved from 1538. Population obviously decreases as you go back in time, which reduces the likelihood of finding more than one possible individual who could be your ancestor. What's more, as already mentioned, the Mormons have indexed nearly all the records contained in parish registers in the IGI. Given that the IGI is not 100 per cent reliable, when searching pre-1837 you really must pay a visit to the parish in question at some point and consult the original registers.

If you don't know where your family was living prior to 1837, start with the search on the IGI. Key in all the information you have about the ancestor and see what comes up. If an IGI search doesn't produce anything (and it usually will), then use the oldest evidence you have from the civil registration records.

For example, you know from the civil registration records that your great-great grandfather was born in 1840. The birth certificate gives the name and address of his father, so your starting point should be the parish of that address. You could take a guesstimate that the father was 28 years old when his child was born, so making his birth year 1812, and start with the parish registers from that year. Again, there's no guarantee that this will be the right parish, as the family could well have moved, but it's a starting point.

A better method still is to use the address of your ancestor in 1840 and look at the Censuses of 1841 and 1831. With luck this should give you the names and ages of everyone in that household, which in turn should enable you to get a more accurate year of birth for your great-great-grandfather. If, for example, you were to see from the 1841 Census record that there was an elder sibling of your great-great-grandfather in the household, say a six-year-old (hence born in 1835), a good first approach would be to look for the baptism of this child, in the parish where the family was living at the time of the 1841 Census.

Priests and parishes

Church of England parish registers will be your primary source for researching pre-1837 records. (Parish records did not cease in 1837, but it's usually easier to go straight to the civil registration registers at this point.) It has been claimed that around 95 per cent of the population of England and Wales in the 1700s was Anglican, so if you are searching for ancestors from around that time you will probably find them in Church of England registers.

From the Middle Ages, England was divided into about 11,000 parishes, each the responsibility of an 'incumbent' – priest, vicar or rector. Parishioners paid tithes – ecclesiastical taxes – to the incumbent for the upkeep of the church and its buildings and sometimes for the care of the poor and sick. Some parishes were tiny and a priest would cover two or three parishes. A county could contain a huge number of parishes. Norfolk, for example, contained 691. Parishes were in turn grouped into dioceses and archdeaconries. The bishops and archdeacons received copies of the registers, in the form of what are known as 'bishops transcripts' (see page 117).

Most parish registers date from 1538. This is when Thomas Cromwell, who was Henry VIII's Vicar-General, ordered that all parish priests keep records of baptisms, marriages and burials in their parish. Unfortunately for genealogists, this does not mean that all parishes now hold perfect, complete registers since 1538. Some priests were more scrupulous than others, and over time registers have been lost or destroyed by fire.

In 1592 it was ordered that registers be made on parchment instead of paper, as the paper was not surviving well. The order also stated that existing pre-1592 entries should be transferred to parchment. Many parishes did not bother, or they just transferred the entries from 1558, when Elizabeth I came to the throne, hoping no one would really care about the 1538–58 period. They seem to have got away with it. Fortunately, however, from the late sixteenth century onwards many registers were deposited with local records offices.

There is another reason why registers may be incomplete. During the English Civil War of 1642–8 many priests fled or were removed from their parish. Often they did not return until as late as 1660. For the period 1653–60 the registration of baptisms, marriages and burials was put into the hands of local officials. They did keep their own books but very few of these have survived. Only civil marriages were allowed, conducted by a Justice of the Peace, and, again, very few of these survive. When Charles I was restored to the throne in 1660 some events were posthumously recorded, but there are considerable gaps. If you are searching for records from around this time, always bear the Civil War and its effects in mind.

How registers were kept

Parish registers are fascinating documents, although you need to be aware of the potential pitfalls. Spelling is often haphazard, dates can make little sense and names seem to change frequently. Early records are particularly tricky because baptisms, marriages and burials were often not separated into different sections, so you could be looking at a page of entries and assuming they are all baptisms when in fact they are a mixture of all three types of event for that particular year.

A register will tell you the surname and Christian name of the person being baptized (or married, or buried), the date of the ceremony and the names of some of their relatives. Addresses are sometimes given but not always. Marriage registers may state whether the person was a widow or widower, and from 1754 the signatures of both spouses should be included (see Hardwicke's Marriage Act, page 121). The amount of information recorded depended on the particular incumbent and this is why the success of your research can vary quite dramatically depending on which parish the records are located in.

In 1598, Parliament passed a law requiring all parish priests to send copies of the registers to the bishops responsible for that area. These are known as 'Bishops Transcripts' and were required to be sent to the bishop each year, within a month of Easter. They contain similar information as the parish register but can be of further use as sometimes bishops supplemented the registers with additional information. Therefore a bishop's transcript can reveal more than the corresponding parish register. They are also good for cross-checking.

There are gaps in the transcripts, particularly for the Civil War period, and some counties have more complete records than others, which probably comes down to the particular whim or accuracy of the bishop. You shouldn't assume that the transcript will be held in the same county as the parish in which the baptism, marriage or burial took place. The seat of the bishop may well have been elsewhere. For example, the parish of Chevening in West Kent was part of the diocese of the Bishop of Canterbury, and the bishop's transcripts are therefore held in Lambeth Palace Library in London. The National Index of Parish Registers (see page 124) will help you locate the whereabouts of bishops' transcripts.

Baptisms

There are a number of things you should be aware of when searching baptismal registers in order to make the identification of your relative as accurate as possible. It's useful to know that for much of the fifteenth, sixteenth, seventeenth and eighteenth centuries births tended to be very regular – families often had very large numbers of children with a two-year gap between each child. Although children were meant to be baptized soon after their birth, it was quite common for families to wait until the next child was born and get them baptized together. You shouldn't therefore assume that two children with the same baptism date are twins.

Neither should you assume that everyone was baptized as a child. Adult baptisms certainly took place, perhaps because a child was born during the Civil War period when priests often fled their parish, and was subsequently baptized when the priest returned. For this reason it's not impossible for the dates of your ancestor's baptism and marriage to be very close.

It was not at all uncommon to find two people with both the same surname and forename within the parish. If the mother's maiden name appears on the baptism register (as we have seen, the amount and nature of information varies considerably, depending on the parish and the date of the entry) then this will help you identify which of the two is your ancestor. Early registers of baptisms (before 1700) will not record the child's mother's maiden name and you will need to find the marriage record in order to obtain this. Fathers and sons with the same name were often called 'senior' or 'junior' and this can help rule out any confusion.

In 1812, Rose's Act was passed, which helped matters considerably. The Act stated that baptismal registers had to include the names of the child's parents, their address and the name of the clergyman conducting the ceremony. What's more, entries had to be made in printed registers, rather than written by hand on parchment. This greatly improved the legibility and organization of the records.

Although all baptisms were supposed to take place in the parish church, private baptisms at home were not uncommon and were usually due to a child being ill and hence too weak to be taken to church. Parish priests often took a fairly relaxed line with such baptisms and sometimes 'received' the child in a later church ceremony. You can tell if your ancestor was baptized privately, as there will be a 'P' or 'Priv' in the margin of the register.

Marriages

Between 1538 and 1754, parish marriage registers contained only the names of the two spouses and the date of the event. Crucially, however, they do give the female's maiden name, helpful if you are researching the female line of that branch of your family. Marriages usually took place in the bride's parish, but often the ceremony was in the nearest city or market town. Banns were called on three consecutive Sundays before the wedding, usually in the village square. The purpose of calling banns was to announce the forthcoming event to the parish and to give any parishioner who may wish to do so the opportunity to voice any objection to the marriage.

During this early period rules were lax. Marriages took place in many types of establishment (London's Fleet prison being a notorious example). Clandestine, runaway marriages and marriages between minors were common, and clergy often conducted irregular marriages in return for a fee (particularly when there was obvious pregnancy) or carried out non-Anglican marriages. This changed in 1753 with the introduction of Hardwicke's Marriage Act.

The Act was introduced as an attempt to put an end to the many irregular marriages in England and Wales and to improve the system of registration. It stated that:

- Marriages must be performed in a parish church in the parish of one of the spouses
- Marriages must be performed by an Anglican clergyman
- There must be two witnesses present
- The marriage must take place after the publication of banns or the issuing of a valid marriage licence
- Minors (boys under 14 and girls under 12) must have parental consent to marry
- The register must be maintained in an organized manner, in chronological and alphabetical order
- The register must contain, in addition to the spouses' names and date of the marriage, the spouses' addresses, their condition (i.e., bachelor, spinster, widow, widower), whether the marriage was by banns or licence and the groom's occupation
- The register must contain the signatures of both spouses, the two witnesses and the clergyman conducting the ceremony.

Occasionally marriages were celebrated twice; once in the bride's parish and once in the groom's parish. You should not therefore assume that two entries denote two different sets of people. If all the details match up then it's quite likely the sign of a double celebration.

Entries for burials are of less interest to the genealogist than those for baptisms and marriages, but the date of a burial can help you guess at a baptism date you cannot find, and will be useful if you are looking for a gravestone.

Mobility

Our ancestors moved around far more than we might think, often over vast distances. In the civil registration period this was often as a result of the industrial revolution, but prior to civil registration movement seems to have been just as frequent, though distances were smaller because transport was not as developed. Movement between neighbouring parishes was particularly high. This is actually good news in terms of finding your ancestors in parish registers. If you cannot find an entry in the place you are expecting to find it, then simply searching the registers of neighbouring parishes will often provide the missing link.

If, for example, you have found the marriage of your great-great-great-great-grandfather and great-great-great-great-grandmother in a particular parish, but cannot find the baptism of their first child, consider checking in neighbouring parishes. It was quite common for a woman to return to her parent's parish for the birth and hence the baptism of the first child. As different generations of families tended to settle in the same area, it's quite likely that you will find the baptism in a neighbouring parish.

In order to search the localities successfully you will need to be armed with maps that show the boundaries of parishes and counties for the period you are investigating. The Institute of Heraldic and Genealogical Studies (see Chapter 7) has a range of these maps and they will facilitate your task considerably.

As well as the appropriate maps, another very important research aid is the National Index of Parish Registers (NIPR). This is held by the Society of Genealogists and gives the location of all parish registers in England and Wales. Local records offices often have copies too.

Using the International Genealogical Index

As I have mentioned, a vast amount of parish registers have been indexed in the IGI – it contains records for over 240 million people across the world and is updated every year. The IGI is held on microfiche at the Census office, the PRO, the SoG and many local records offices. It's a great place to start when researching the pre-1837 period and is particularly good where families have moved around a lot between parishes. However, the IGI can *never* be a substitute for searching the original parish records, only a starting point.

The information in the IGI is generally taken from parish registers and bishops' transcripts. The IGI is a fantastic finding aid, but you should bear the following in mind when you are using it to trace relatives.

The IGI concentrates primarily on baptisms. Entries for marriages and burials are not comprehensive

- Not all counties or parishes have been indexed. The Parish and Vital Records List (PVRL), which is part of the IGI, will tell you whether the area you are interested in is included. Not all periods for every parish have been indexed. If a family suddenly appears in the records, it may be that the records are incomplete rather than that they have moved. Again, you should refer to the PVRL.
- The IGI is indexed alphabetically by surname and then by forename. However, variations on names are lumped together, such as Law and Laws, so you need to search quite carefully and run your eye down the complete list of names starting 'Law' to be sure you have covered all possibilities
- Baptisms, marriages and births are not separated.
- Names are indexed as they appear in the original parish registers. Therefore variations on a name, such as Wm for William, will not appear with its full version. For example, there will be several other forenames between William and Wm (eg. Winston), so you will need to search for both types. Similarly, commonly used variations, such as Jack for John and

Peggy for Margaret, will be a long long way apart in the index. The FamilySearch database addresses this problem by giving you the option to search by similar name rather than exact name, so that variations are automatically retrieved.

- Relationships are not always specified.
- Transcription errors inevitably occur. With an index of 240 million names, it cannot be error-free. Sometimes the original registers are difficult to decipher and hence transcription is hampered. The IGI is an international index and it may be that transcribers are not of English mother tongue.

Boyd's Marriage Index

Percival Boyd indexed over 6 million names from the registers of 4,300 parishes for the period 1538–1837. This enormous index is very useful as a supplement to the IGI, since the latter concentrates primarily on baptisms. Boyd's Marriage Index by no means covers all parishes in a particular county, or even all counties, but it may still provide the information you are looking for and have been unable to find in the marriage register, particularly if your ancestors moved to neighbouring parishes. Marriages are indexed under the names of both spouses, so you do not need to know both names in order to search. The original manuscript pages are held at the SoG and many local records offices hold copies.

County indexes

As with civil registration, many local records offices, county councils, family history societies or individuals have dedicated themselves to compiling indexes of local parish registers. Cambridgeshire Family History Society, for example, has a complete index of baptisms that took place between 1801 and 1837 in Cambridgeshire. Others have fairly complete marriage registers. Bedfordshire takes first prize here. Bedfordshire County Council has transcribed and indexed every single entry from the original parish registers for baptisms, marriages and burials from 1538-1812. If your ancestors are from Bedfordshire, then you're onto a winner. This voluntary indexing is ongoing – check with your local records office to find out exactly what has been indexed for your area.

A personal visit

As we have seen, there are many ways of gaining access to copies of and indexes to parish registers without actually physically visiting the parish in question. However, there will come a point when only an inspection of the original parish register will provide the certainty you are looking for. What's more, as you research your family further you are sure to feel a pull towards the place where they grew up and lived. The desire to visit churchyards to look at gravestones is often a strong one, particularly when you can see a whole series of your ancestors' gravestones arranged in a family group.

If you decide to make a personal visit then you will need to contact the priest or vicar of the parish and bear in mind his or her other parochial commitments – Sundays are not a great time for a visit! It's best to phone first and arrange a specific time. You will probably be supervised as you look through the register – register books have been known to be defaced or pages torn out – and you may be expected to pay a small fee.

It's worth preparing as meticulously as you can, so that you don't waste either the vicar's or your own time.

Make sure you know exactly what you are looking for, that you have done as much preparatory research using the IGI and/or local indexes as possible, and that you have all the notebooks, cross-referencing documents and other files you will need.

If you do not know the parish you may want to stay overnight. This will give you a chance to explore church gravestones (and perhaps those of neighbouring parishes too), visit the local history museum if there is one, explore second-hand bookshops and even talk to locals. First-hand experience is important to bring your research alive – years spent searching indexes in libraries could make your quest a somewhat sterile experience.

Stumbling blocks

No matter how well you have researched, there are still several reasons why you may fail to find an entry in the parish registers.

1. Illiteracy. You are dealing with a period of history when many people could not read or write. A man might know how to spell his own name, but not those of all his children. Nicknames and abbreviations were often used. The name on a baptism record may be 'Clark', but on a marriage record 'Clarke'. Yet you cannot assume this is not one and the same person.

2. **Handwriting.** Most sixteenth- and seventeenth-century registers were written in a hand known as 'secretary script'. This takes some getting used to but is not hard to decipher. Basically it's a question of distinguishing between f and s, c and r and C and T. Latin was also frequently used. This is a less insurmountable problem than it might seem. Names of months and days of the week are easy to recognize, as the names we use today are derived from Latin anyway. Dates are in numerals so there's no problem there. Names are the only tricky area – Charles would be written as Carolus, John as Johannes, for example. You could enlist the help of a specialist in this field but people are often surprised at how little assistance they actually need when faced with Latin script.

3. **Infant mortality.** Some historians claim that in the late 1700s over 50 per cent of the children born in large cities died before they reached the age of five. If

you find a baptism, and then the name seems to disappear from the registers, infant mortality may be the reason. Many children were stillborn and did not even make it to the baptismal register. And of course it was not unusual for mothers to die in childbirth.

4. **Priests often wrote the entries in note form in rough books and later transcribed them into the register.** Similarly, they sometimes used loose sheets that were later bound together. The potential for error here is easy to see. Some rough books survive in local records offices and are worth consulting.

5. **The legal ages for marriage were just twelve for a girl and fourteen for a boy.** This seems incredibly young to us today. If you are going by today's standards you may in fact be looking too far back for a marriage. In reality it could be just twelve years after the baptism.

6. **Illegitimacy.** If a child was illegitimate, then the baptism certificate will only record the mother's name. There may simply be no way of finding the father.

7. **Stamp duty tax.** This was a charge introduced on baptisms in 1783. It was withdrawn in 1794 and it

seems that some parents waited until the repeal of the tax before having their children baptized.

8. **Burial registers will not list anyone who died at sea or who was declared a heretic, committed suicide, or was not baptized.**

9. **Non-parochial registers.** The baptism, marriage or burial may not have taken place in the parish church, but in a hospital, workhouse, court, cathedral, or abroad. The NIPR includes indexes to non-parochial registers and this should be your first port of call.

Searching for non-conformist ancestors

From the Middle Ages to the Reformation, the majority (90–95 per cent) of English people were C of E and hence baptized, married and buried in Anglican parishes. However, if you know or suspect that your ancestors were from other religious denominations, then you will need to investigate other specific sources to trace your family. There is not room here to go into these records in detail but I can show you where to go to research further.

By non-conformist we mean dissenting Protestants (Baptists, Methodists, Presbyterians, Quakers) as well as Roman Catholics and Jews. For the period after 1837 there is no difficulty in researching a non-conformist family, as civil registration demanded that all religious persuasions record their births, marriages and deaths in the national registers. The pre-1837 period is more problematical. This is not to say that Anglican parishes never performed non-Anglican ceremonies. They frequently did, and from 1754 Hardwicke's Marriage Act ruled that all denominations (except Quakers) should conduct their marriages in an Anglican parish church. Non-conformist burials often took place in Anglican churchyards too, but a non-conformist ceremony was not permitted until 1880. Consequently many non-conformists established their own burial grounds, such as Bunhill Fields in London, whose registers are held at the PRO.

Religious intolerance in many ways defined society in the Middle Ages, much as it does today. If you need to search non-conformist records to find your ancestors, you will be made acutely aware of this. Roman Catholics were burnt at the stake as recently as 1611. Discrimination became gradually less severe (the 1689 Act of Toleration allowed citizens to attend churches other than the parish church if they swore allegiance to and belief in the Holy Trinity), but non-conformists could not hold government office or enter Oxford or Cambridge until well into the 1700s. Jews could not vote before 1835.

Your search for non-conformist ancestors is made much easier by the Non-Parochial Register Act of 1840, which stated that all pre-1837 non-conformist registers should be deposited with the Registrar General. These are now held at the PRO. Not all registers were deposited, however.

Sources

Many non-conformist records survive. Most sources will be familiar to you already from chapters 3, 4 and 5, but other sources are peculiar to the denomination in question. The NIPR is a useful starting point when attempting to locate the whereabouts of any non-conformist register. The following information on sources may also help.

Roman Catholics

Roman Catholics were persecuted perhaps more than any other group in England from the Reformation to the early 1900s. Priests were sometimes jailed or executed. Nevertheless, some Catholic baptisms, marriages and burials did take place in Anglican churches – often this depended on the particular scruples of the priest concerned – and so appear in the Anglican parish registers. Sometimes Catholics were buried at night in Anglican graveyards, so that friends could conduct the ceremony in secret. Marriages may have taken place in a 'mission', or unofficial chapel.

The Catholic Church did require its priests to keep records of baptisms, marriages and burials, but it seems many did not do so. The records of itinerant priests, who travelled over large areas of the country conducting Catholics ceremonies, are particularly difficult to find.

Persecution of Roman Catholics meant a large number of fines, levies, taxes and land seizure. Records of all these can be found at the PRO. The NIPR records the whereabouts of all the different Catholic missions, as well as the location of burial grounds. The Catholic Record

Society is another useful port of call – it holds many Catholic registers and publishes a number of useful indexes and journals.

Presbyterians

The Presbyterian movement began within the Church of England. Its aim was to abolish many of the rituals that were part and parcel of Anglican worship. The movement was strongest in Scotland but gained ground in England during the Civil War; by the mid-1800s, there were about 200,000 practising Presbyterians. Later they became know as Unitarians, and the United Reformed Church was established in 1972. Following the Non-Parochial Register Act of 1840 most Presbyterian registers were deposited with the Registrar General. The United Reformed Church Historical Society may well be able to help you with tracing earlier ancestors.

Quakers

The Quakers, founded in the seventeenth century by George Fox, have also long been persecuted for their beliefs. They refused to join the armed forces, pay tithes or attend Anglican services. The good news for genealogists is that Quakers loved meetings – weekly meetings, monthly meetings, quarterly meetings, annual meetings, women's meetings – and always kept meticulous minutes of the proceedings. The Quakers developed their own registration system for births (they did not practise baptism), marriages and burials, and these records were in fact recognized by the Anglican Church (which explains why Quakers were exempt from Hardwicke's Marriage Act). These registers are now held at the PRO, together with their indexes.

Because of the penchant of the Quakers for recording any life event, research of Quaker records can be very fruitful. As well as the PRO you should investigate the records of the Library of the Society of Friends (173–177 Euston Road, London NW1 2BJ). It holds details of many monthly meetings, wills, taxation and education records and a range of other publications.

Baptists

Baptists believe that baptisms should only take place when a person is of adult age, as before that time the person cannot make an informed judgement on whether they wish to be baptized. The movement began in the seventeenth century and flourished over the following 100 years. As with other non-conformists, pre-1837 records were deposited with the Registrar General in 1840 – copies are held at the SoG. Other useful sources are the PRO (which holds many Baptist burial registers), local records offices, archives of Baptist churches and colleges, Regent's Park College in Oxford, the Strict Baptist Historical Society's Library in Dunstable and the Gospel Standard Baptist Library in Hove.

Methodists

The Methodist movement was founded in 1740 by John Wesley, Charles Wesley and George Whitefield. Over the next century it splintered into many groups. Records before the early 1800s can be difficult to trace; it seems that few have survived. In 1818, however, a Methodist General Registry was established to record all Methodist births and baptisms. Some earlier entries were retrospectively included. This Registry, along with records of Methodist burial grounds, is held by the PRO and by some local records offices. Other useful sources for finding Methodist ancestors are the Methodist Archives and Research Centre (at the John Rylands Library in Manchester), the Wesley Historical Society and the Museum of Methodism at Wesley's Chapel (both in London).

Dr Williams's Library

In 1742, partly to make up for the casual approach to record keeping by many non-conformist ministers, a General Register of Births of Children of Protestant Dissenters was set up by one Dr Williams. This register is held at 14 Gordon Square, London WC1, and contains nearly 50,000 records of births. Parents paid a small fee to have their children recorded there (they had to provide evidence of the birth from at least two sources, such as the midwife and a witness) and in exchange received a certificate confirming the registration of the birth. The register was closed in 1837, when civil registration for England and Wales came into force. Dr Williams's Library can therefore be a very useful resource where local records are sporadic, or even non-existent.

Jews

The history of persecution of the Jews in England is a long one and hence records of baptisms, marriages and deaths, particularly from the Middle Ages, are patchy. Jews were banished from England in 1290 and only permitted to return in 1655. Synagogues started appearing from 1690, but discrimination was still considerable right into the 1900s. The Jewish population in England grew from about 600 in the late 1600s to 250,000 by the 1920s.

One of the reasons Jewish ancestry can be difficult to trace is that many Jews anglicized their names (or changed them completely) when they arrived in England, for fear of persecution. It may be worth doing a bit of research on this topic – the journal *Avotaynu: The International Review of Jewish Genealogy* has featured numerous articles on how surnames were changed. Other difficulties are that records are usually in Hebrew (existing relatives may be able to help), and correspond to the Jewish calendar, which is about 3,760 years ahead of the British one. Careful calculations when assessing birth dates are therefore required.

The good news is that there are numerous archives and libraries that can help with your research. Synagogue records (there are now over 400 synagogues in Britain) are particularly helpful. They hold minutes of council meetings and registers of members. If you know where your ancestors lived, then the local synagogue is quite likely to hold some relevant information about your family. Other useful sources are the Anglo-Jewish archives (most of which are held at the SoG), the London Museum of Jewish Life, the Jewish Refugee Committee and the Jewish Historical Society. Many Jewish newspapers are well established; the best known is the *Jewish Chronicle*, first published in 1941. The British Newspaper Library at Colindale, North London holds back copies of this and other Jewish newspapers.

CHAPTER 6

GENEALOGY
ON THE
INTERNET

One of the first questions of the beginner family-tree researcher may well be 'Can I do it all on the Internet?' The short answer is 'no'. The longer answer is 'Well, you can find out a huge amount on the Internet, but at some point you will have to go to the original sources. For the moment, at least.'

The harsh reality is that there are very few first-hand resources on the Internet – by this I mean original transcripts of parish registers, original birth certificates, etc. It is quite likely that one day all these documents will be available online but it's a huge project and a tricky one, given the delicate nature of much of this material.

At the moment, all material on the Internet is second-hand – it has been transcribed from the original sources, and as with all transcriptions, contains the possibility of error. What's more, much of the information on the Web could be described as third-hand – individuals have taken secondary sources, such as the IGI, and created their own website devoted to their own family tree from this. The possibilities of error are therefore doubled. The census is the closest we get to having first-hand documents online at the moment – the 1901 Census became available online in early 2002 and earlier censuses are in the process of being digitized too.

The absence of first-hand documents on the Web means that any research you do here should always be backed up at some point by a consultation with the originals. However, genealogy on the Internet does have the following two absolutely crucial advantages over non-virtual research.

Firstly, it is international. Obviously this is a major plus point if you know or suspect that your ancestors either lived abroad or moved around a lot between countries. The Web gives you access to genealogical information from a large number of countries around the world – this type of research would be pretty much impossible if you had to visit the original sources, unless you had an inordinate amount of time on your hands and plenty of money for air fares. Of course, the fact still remains that you must consult the original sources at some point, but you can certainly get a long way on the Web.

Secondly, it can save you a huge amount of time and frustration. Consulting the websites of the organizations, records offices, libraries and museums you wish to visit enables you to learn exactly what is there, how it is organized, and even the file number of the material you need to consult. This is a major advantage with somewhere like the PRO, whose resources can be quite overwhelming. If you just turn up without having found out what is there first, you will be completely daunted and may spend an afternoon getting absolutely nowhere. By visiting the PRO's website first (see page 152) you can browse through the different sections, identify the area of the organization you need to visit and be well prepared to get the most out of it when you actually get there.

Practical considerations

If you think you are going to be spending a lot of time searching genealogical records online, then it's worth thinking about how you are being charged for your online time. If you are currently on a rate that allows you free online time at evenings and weekends, and you are in a full-time job, then this may suit you fine. However, it's probably worth considering a package that gives you unlimited online time (for a monthly fee). You may intend to be strict with yourself but it's surprising how quickly time can fly once you get going. You should maximize opportunities to 'browse offline' too.

Because of the nature of genealogical websites – i.e., they often hold extraordinarily large amounts of data – researching can be slow. This will also affect your costs. Keep a look out for whether or not the services offered by a site are free or not. For example, FamilySearch (the IGI) is free, but you won't get far with Origins before being asked for your credit card details.

Featured sites

The rest of this chapter looks at different areas of family-history research and lists some websites you might find useful when tracing your family tree. You'll already be familiar with many of the organizations listed here – all the big genealogical bodies, such as the SoG, PRO, IGI and FFHS, have websites, often containing similar information. As you start surfing, you'll soon find that the same sites come up time and time again, as you use the 'links' to navigate forward and back between the sites of complementary organizations.

As we are dealing here with information that is in many cases being modified daily, it's impossible to be absolutely up-to-date. In any case, there's only so much a book can tell you about websites – you've really just got to get on there and explore for yourself. Oh yes, and every site must have a picture of a tree on its home page – absolutely obligatory!

For starters

www.genuki.com

There's no reason why you shouldn't use the Web as a learning tool as well as a searching aid. GENUKI (the UK and Ireland Genealogical Information Service) is a site that tells you everything you need to know about getting started in family tree research (you can't get more basic than 'What is genealogy?') and covers much of the background contained in Chapter 1 of this book. With GENUKI you should be able to go from a position of complete ignorance with regard to family trees to an actual search via the many links to other sites (such as FamilySearch and Cyndi's List – see below). Other beginner's sites are **www.rootsweb.com** and **www.gengateway.com**, though the latter tends to concentrate on US records.

Do-it-all

The websites of the main genealogical organizations contain a vast amount of information and allow you to learn everything you could want to know about the individual organizations themselves as well as about pretty much every different aspect of genealogy. I believe I am right in saying that at present only FamilySearch, the online version of the Mormon's IGI, is a facility for finding the actual baptism, marriage or burial records of your ancestors (though of course these are not the originals). However, most of the other sites do offer a surname search and provide links to family history societies or to individuals that are researching particular names or geographical regions. Really these websites are signposts, pointing you in the way of libraries, record centres, or individuals in any part of the world who may have a family link with you.

Other things you can do via these other sites include purchasing books and merchandise related to every aspect of genealogy and finding out what is available in their respective libraries and finding out which local records offices and history societies are near you. You can also read reviews of books and journals, hear about forthcoming events and swap information with other researchers via message boards or e-mail. The sites that will be central to your research are:

www.familysearch.org

This is the FamilySearch Internet Genealogy Service, or in other words, the online version of the Mormon's huge IGI database. Searching for your ancestors is pretty simple – you don't need to fill in any more than a surname for a valid search. Obviously, though, you could end up with huge amounts of records this way, and the search will necessarily be slow. See Chapter 5 for details on how to search the IGI database. Numerous features of this website include an online tour of the huge family history library in Salt Lake City.

www.cyndislist.com

Run by American family history obsessive Cyndi Howells, this is an encyclopedia of over 80,000 genealogy websites. If you have a genealogy question, Cyndi will have the answer. It's truly international and though supremely American in style, there is no real US bias in the information contained. Again, a massive site, so it can be slow to navigate.

www.familyrecords.gov.uk

This is the site of the Family Records Centre. It's incredibly clear and well laid-out, much like the Family Records Centre itself, and details every last one of the different types of records held at 1 Myddelton Street in London. Not only does the site cover all pre- and post-1837 sources, but it also contains valuable information on how to trace adoptive parents and immigrants. The 1901 Census online can be accessed from this site, or directly by going to **www.census.pro.gov.uk**.

www.pro.gov.uk

The Family Record Centre's sister website, **www.pro.gov.uk** details all the records held at the Public Records Office in Kew. It's particularly important to consult this site before visiting Kew, to have at least some idea of where you will find the type of information you are seeking in this vast record centre. Understanding the index is quite a feat in itself. Do your initial research online rather than at the library. The PRO and FRC websites have a great deal of information about Scottish and Northern Irish records, as well as for England and Wales.

www.sog.org.uk

This is the site of the Society of Genealogists. The library is probably the Society's most impressive resource – it has over 9,000 Parish Registers, County Records, Census material, Poll Books and Directories. The website **www.sog.org.uk** gives good tips on how to best prepare for a visit to this huge library.

www.ffhs.org.uk

This is the site of the Federation of Family History Societies, the umbrella organization for the 200 or so Family History Societies in the United Kingdom. The site explains the work of the FHS and puts you in e-mail contact with researchers in your local area, or the specific area you might be interested in. It also includes contact details for societies in Ireland, overseas and for one-name societies.

www.genealogy.com

This is one of the major sites in the United States, but it does also contain international data. It links straight to Family Treemaker (see Chapter 7) and allows you to do an online search for your ancestors. It has links to the Social Security Death Index (for the US) and to telephone directories. One of its most interesting features is the Virtual Cemetery, where you can post an electronic memorial message, together with a photo of your ancestor.

www.earl.org.uk/familia

Familia is an extremely useful site to the genealogist – a continually updated online directory of all the family history to be found in public libraries in the United Kingdom. The Library Association is a partner and many of the main genealogy websites, such as those of the Family Records Centre and Public Records Office, have links to Familia.

www.origins.net

This is mainly a site confined to Scottish records, but it is shortly due to take over the records of the Society of Genealogists, which will make Origins a vast, international site.

Searching for names

As mentioned, most of the above sites will give you the opportunity to perform an online name search, but there are also a number of specialist sites for this and your best bet is to start with these.

www.rootsweb.com

This is the Web's oldest free name search site. You can search by name or a location. It is fairly US-biased but has some interesting information, including the option to search royal lineages online. Roots Web also hosts the World Genweb project (**www.worldgenweb.org**) which is run by volunteers. The idea is to create a genealogical databank for every country of the world, with a volunteer in each country, who is familiar with that country's resources, responsible for maintaining online information. The downside is that some countries are still without a volunteer and the information is only as accurate as the individual responsible for the page. However, it could be invaluable, particularly if you are interested in small countries not covered by other sites.

www.one-name.org

This is the site of the Guild of One-name Studies (GOONS) and, as befitting the Guild, the site is quite pleased with itself. It tells you all you need to know about becoming a member and links you to the websites or e-mail addresses of individual researchers.

Military

The following sites will be useful if you are researching ancestors who served in the forces, but all play second fiddle to the PRO at Kew (see page 152), which should be your first port of call for any British Navy, British Army, Royal Marines or Merchant Navy records.

www.iwm.org.uk

The Imperial War Museum's site.

www.cwgc.org

The Commonwealth War Graves Commission's site.

www.mod.uk

The Ministry of Defence's site.

www.rememberingthebattleofbritain.co.uk

The remembering project – a site devoted to compiling Second World War memories and to commemorating victims of the Holocaust.

Royal and heraldic sites

The fascination many people have for finding out whether there is any royal blood in their family (and at some point in time there almost certainly will have been) is well attended to on the Internet. Looking for family coats of arms or crests is a similarly popular genealogical pursuit. There are a number of specialist sites devoted exclusively to these aspects of genealogy:

www.baronage.co.uk

This is the online presence of the Baronage Press, which publishes books and journals on how to trace connections with noble lines. The magazine *The Baronage* and newsletter *The Feudal Herald* can be accessed online. The site goes out of its way to warn you about the many royal genealogy scam merchants out there, offering you false coats of arms and titles.

www.worldroots.com

This is a vast database of Europe's royal dynasties set up by Brigitte Gastel-Lloyd, whose own royal lineage features on the site. It contains the lineages of royal and aristocratic families such as the Hapsburgs and the Medicis, and shows all the descendants of Queen Victoria to the present day, among many other royal lines. Nobility as well as royalty is covered.

www.college-of-arms.gov.uk

The restrained tone of this site complements the nature of the College of Arms very well. You can find out all about this historical organization and link to sites such as those of the House of Lords, the British Library and the British monarchy. The College of Arms is a great place for the beginner in heraldry. Go to Frequently Asked Questions for the answers to heraldry basics such as 'Do coats of arms belong to surnames?' and 'What is a crest?', and find out how you can have a coat or crest identified.

www.ihgs.ac.uk

This is the website of the Institute of Heraldic and Genealogical Studies. As is to be expected of an educational body, there is information on courses leading to the Diploma in Genealogy and the

Licentiateship of the Institute. The IHGS's remit is wide – the site includes information on the Institute's research into hereditary aspects of conditions such as Alzheimer's and schizophrenia.

And last but not least…

www.royal.gov.uk

The website of the British Monarchy. Not of great use to the genealogist, but it does tell you why the Queen keeps Corgis.

Research services

If you simply don't have the time to do all your family research yourself, and we have seen what a time-consuming activity genealogy can be, then why not get a professional researcher to help you out? The web is a great place to look for research services. If you are looking for one-to-one help you will generally have to pay for it. Most researchers will give you an estimate if you explain exactly what you hope they can achieve for you. It's up to you to weigh up whether you think this service will be worthwhile overall. The major factor will probably be how easy it is for you to access the information yourself, and whether the research would involve the travel and accommodation costs of a trip to a local parish, for example.

Another useful service offered by individual researchers is a courier service to and from major record centres, for example to pick up birth certificates that you have previously ordered from the Family Records Centre.

Your first stop should probably be AGRA (**www.agra.org.uk**). This is the website of the Association of Genealogists and Record Agents. It's impossible to list all the local researchers that could be of use to you, but AGRA is a good starting point to find someone specializing in the county, town or village you are interested in. It's a pretty safe bet that any researcher you find via AGRA will be competent – all members have to comply with AGRA's Code of Practice, details of which you'll find on the site. The subject index of members' special interests its quite an eye opener and proof if ever it were needed of the breadth of the subject of genealogy.

www.gendocs.demon.co.uk

GenDocs is an example of a site that offers a daily courier service to deliver and collect documents for you from the Family Records Centre, London Metropolitan Archives and Guildhall Library, among others.

www.geocities.com/Heartland/Plains/8555

The Look-Up Exchange is a courier service with a difference, by which individuals volunteer to consult records that they can easily access, either from their own reference works or proximity to a local records office, free of charge. The site has e-mail addresses of all such volunteers nationwide.

Miscellaneous sites

These sites sell magazines, journals and books online, as well as offering the content of the publications online, in the majority of cases. And there's also the UK BDM Exchange, which didn't seem to fit in to any other category very well!

www.family-tree.co.uk

This is the website of *Family Tree Magazine*, which is without a doubt the leading publication on genealogy in the United Kingdom. A subscription to *Family Tree Magazine* is almost certainly the best way to keep absolutely up-to-date with developments both in genealogical research and in the indexing, availability and digitizing of both local and national records. This attractive, uncluttered site gives summaries of all the wide-ranging articles in the current and back issues of both *Family Tree Magazine* and its sister publication, *Practical Family History*.

www.jodenoy.clare.net/genbooks/main.htm

Jodenoy books is linked to the huge book website amazon.co.uk and enables you to search and order almost any genealogical title in print, including published parish registers, of which there are hundreds, potentially saving you a lengthy journey. There are a number of links to other useful genealogy online bookstores.

www.mmpublications.co.uk

From this site you can order microfiche copies of many directories and indexes from the early 1700s to the present day. Examples of directories available are Kelly's, Post Office directories, Owners of Land indexes and military records such as Hart's Navy Lists and lists of East India Company employees. Most of the lists only cost a few pounds to order and could save you a long trawl through the microfilms in a library or local record office.

www.onlinegenealogy.com

This is the site of the *Journal of Online Genealogy*. All the periodical's articles can be read online. An interesting feature of the site is 'Genealogy's Most Wanted', which puts researchers who have reached a brick wall in contact with other researchers who may be able to help.

www.ukbdm.org.uk/

The BDM Exchange is a fascinating site that takes you right to the original documents for births, marriages and deaths in this country. It is a free information exchange site that puts you in touch with other researchers and tells you which original certificates they hold. A listing might look like this:

CLAYTON William 06/04/1854 Wigan Lancs
ivannet@1earth.net

It is very likely there will be someone somewhere researching the same ancestors as you, and with this site you can get direct access to the information on the original certificate without ordering from the FRC (and, of course, get in contact with a potential relation on the way). The idea has obviously caught on. Just a quick search brought up similar BDM Exchange pages for Scotland, Ireland, Benelux, France, Germany, USA, Australasia, Canada, Russia and even Cuba.

International sites

All the sites so far listed are international, in that they either hold records for a large number of countries or at least link to sites that do. The following sites, however, provide specific information about and links to records held in a particular country. This quickens your search. Of course there are many more than are listed here, but I've picked out those of the countries closest to England geographically (Wales, Scotland, Northern Ireland and Ireland), and also historically (Commonwealth countries and countries from which large numbers emigrated to England). These websites go someway towards addressing the difficulties of searching for information on immigrant ancestors, or for those who spent long periods settled in a Commonwealth country such as Australia.

Wales

www.celtic-connect.demon.co.uk

Celtic Connect is a Welsh ancestry site. As we know, Wales is included in the civil registration records, but this is a more specialist site and particularly useful for pre-1837 records and searching for surnames. Its size makes it much quicker to search than some of the huge international databases.

Scotland

We've looked at Origins Net, which is probably the best starting point for Scottish records. Other useful sites are: **www.scotweb.co.uk**and **www.scotlandsclans.com.**

Northern Ireland

http://proni.nics.gov.uk

This is the PRO for Northern Ireland – the PRONI. It holds central and local government records, as well as some owned by private individuals. The actual birth, marriage and death certificates for Northern Ireland are kept by Northern Ireland's General Register Office. PRONI has a link to this site.

Ireland

www.ifhf.org

The Irish Family History Forum is actually operated from New York, perhaps not such a surprise given the history of population movement between these two countries.

www.nationalarchives.ie

The main purpose of this site is to tell you exactly what records are held at the National Archives of Ireland in Dublin which will help you prepare for a research visit.

Australia

www.alphalink.com.au/~aigs/

One of a number of useful Australian sites. A major advantage of this one is that you can actually search some indexes online, such as the Certificates of Freedom 1823–69 of Convicts Transported to Australia and the New South Wales BDM Index.

www.shipping.cohsoft.com.au/afhc

A comprehensive Australian site with surname search, links to researchers, where to find just about any genealogical information in Australia and links to other Australian sites.

Canada

www.archives.ca

This is the site of the National Archives of Canada. There's a search tool called ArchiviaNet that enables you to search by theme or document, and comprehensive information on what is held by the National Archives.

West Indies and Jamaica

www.jamaicanfamilysearch.com

This is a comprehensive site containing the Jamaica Almanac (the Jamaican equivalent of the census, from 1801), military and civil lists, registers and wills, and a surname search. However, you can only search samples for free online – a subscription charge must be paid if you wish to carry out an actual online search.

www.candoo.com/genresources/index.html

A site covering all the Caribbean islands, with details on where microfilm records and registers for each island are, and information on archives, museums and individuals.

India and Pakistan

There is much information available on the Web on searching records in these countries, but, as far as I can see at the time of writing, there are no direct sites. Instead, you need to use some of the big ones, such as Roots Web or Cyndi's List. From there you can go to the section for the country in question and you'll find plenty of information exchange forums, details of records and publications and contacts for people looking for similar names.

Jewish

www.jgsgb.ort.org/

We've already talked about researching Jewish ancestry in Chapter 6. If you're using the Web for your initial research, then this is the best place to start. There's plenty of material to search online, including the JGSGB Index of Marriages from 1897 to 1907, and deaths from 1790. The photograph gallery is a fascinating feature.

You may come across some resistance from other family-tree researchers when it comes to genealogy online. Many of the most recent and most comprehensive books I have read give the Web just a passing mention. This is understandable. If you have devoted your life to dissecting records, visiting parishes, hunting down wills or scouring local archives, and sharing with less enlightened souls the fruits of your research and lifelong passion, then the Web can seem, well, just a bit too easy. Almost like cheating. For the beginner, though, it is fantastic. Such reservations are justified to a certain extent, in that they highlight the unreliability of much Web information, but they also betray a rather pointless unwillingness to exploit the Web and all it has to offer. There are many potential converts out there.

CHAPTER 7

DRAWING YOUR FAMILY TREE

Now that you've done all the hard work, you can finally draw your tree and see the fruits of your labour presented in a satisfying manner. And I mean 'draw' in the broadest sense. Gone are the days when you'd need to have several walls of your living room covered with paper in order to display your tree; today, the most common way of 'drawing' your tree is with the aid of a computer program designed specifically for the purpose.

Electronic family trees have two huge advantages over their hand-drawn variant: first, you can get more information on a page and, second, you can edit it. Working electronically means you can choose the style and size of font to use, and can make sure all individuals of the same generation line up neatly. On paper you'd be wrestling with rulers, pencils and erasers, and would never be able to fit the same amount of information on the tree, let alone keep it neat and easy to follow. An electronic tree also means you can fill in missing information as you go, simply by typing it in, and you can correct errors easily. Family-tree researchers are constantly discovering new information. It may be that a living relation had given you a female ancestor's maiden name, from memory, but when you searched the official records you realized that your relation had misspelt it. If you have already hand-drawn your tree, then modifying such information is a huge headache.

In short, you'd be mad not to exploit the family-tree software available, at least for your first attempt. If you feel the need to draw a tree to fulfil a creative impulse, and there's no doubt there's something immensely satisfying about the pencil and ruler approach that a computer program just cannot provide, then I'd suggest you pick one particular section of your overall tree, and concentrate on getting that as neat and accurate as you can, before tackling a bigger section.

The basics

As space is always at a premium when creating your tree, there are a number of commonly used abbreviations that you will come across in just about any hand-drawn or electronic tree:

born	b.
died	d.
married	= or m.
daughter	dau
son	s.
widow	wid.
widower	wdr.
infant	inf.
baptism/baptized	bap.
burial/buried	bur.

The information for each individual is generally limited to place and date of birth, marriage and death. Occupation is sometimes given. Of course, it's up to you how much information you present. Some people like to write a potted history next to each ancestor, and perhaps attach a photograph – this is really only possible if you are concentrating on a small portion of your tree (a 'mini tree'). Photographic trees are often used to show a likeness passing down through the generations, and as such are a very immediate and powerful visual reminder of your family history.

Drawing your family tree

Marriage is usually shown by an equals sign, and the wife is referred to by her maiden name. Twins are shown by further division of a descending line, as in this diagram:

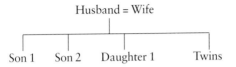

If a parent has children with two spouses, an equals sign is put between the three people and the children of each couple are shown as descending branches. Illegitimate children are often indicated by a dotted line.

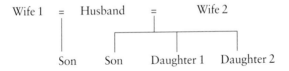

There are several ways of displaying ascendancy and descendancy trees. Some examples are shown below. Ascendancy and descendancy trees are both sometimes called pedigrees.

An hourglass tree is one that combines both ancestors and descendants; for example, a chart showing you at the centre with your parents and grandparents above and your children and grandchildren below. Below is my ascendancy tree over four generations.

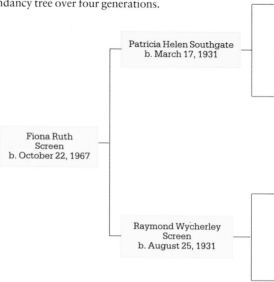

Patricia Helen Southgate
b. March 17, 1931

Fiona Ruth
Screen
b. October 22, 1967

Raymond Wycherley
Screen
b. August 25, 1931

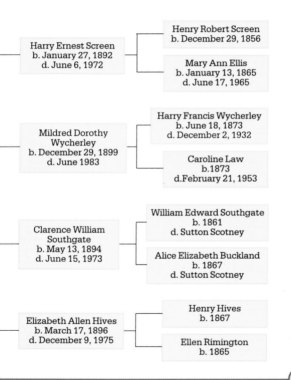

Harry Ernest Screen
b. January 27, 1892
d. June 6, 1972

Henry Robert Screen
b. December 29, 1856

Mary Ann Ellis
b. January 13, 1865
d. June 17, 1965

Mildred Dorothy
Wycherley
b. December 29, 1899
d. June 1983

Harry Francis Wycherley
b. June 18, 1873
d. December 2, 1932

Caroline Law
b.1873
d.February 21, 1953

Clarence William
Southgate
b. May 13, 1894
d. June 15, 1973

William Edward Southgate
b. 1861
d. Sutton Scotney

Alice Elizabeth Buckland
b. 1867
d. Sutton Scotney

Elizabeth Allen Hives
b. March 17, 1896
d. December 9, 1975

Henry Hives
b. 1867

Ellen Rimington
b. 1865

Family Treemaker

The tree above was created with a software package called Family Treemaker. This is by far the most popular brand of genealogical software and it is simple to use. If you have Internet access, then you can go straight to the website at **www.familytreemaker.com** and have a go. Otherwise you can order it from S&N Genealogy Services (Mail Order), Greenacres, Salisbury Road, Chilmark, Wiltshire, SP3 5AH, UK or buy it from the Society of Genealogists or Family Records Centre if you are London-based.

As soon as you access the website, you'll be taken to a screen that allows you to start keying in the details about your family. For each individual you'll have an edit box and be asked to enter all the information you know about that individual. Don't worry if you get something wrong or mistype, just click on the individual again and re-edit. It is a large program so inevitably it can be quite slow, but if you're comparing it with a hand-drawn tree then there's clearly no contest. It took me about twenty minutes to create a tree of four generations. You can save and print your tree for no charge, or buy Family Treemaker on a monthly trial to see if you like it.

Drawing your family tree

One of the most satisfying things about the software is that it allows you to experiment with different ways of displaying information. If you want to concentrate on a mini tree, say just three generations of a female line, then you can add a potted history in the edit box for each individual and this still fits easily on to a sheet of A4 paper. From the tree of four generations I created, I can then click on an individual and choose a new adaptation of the main tree. I can click on Harry Ernest Screen and choose Descendancy in the View option, to give the following mini-tree. This takes only a few seconds.

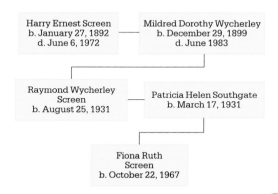

Or you can display your tree by way of an index, which the software sorts into alphabetical rather than birth date order. This is done with just one click of the mouse: choose the View option and click on Index of Individuals.

Name	Birth Date
Buckland, Alice Elizabeth	1867
Ellis, Mary Ann	January 13, 1865
Hives, Elizabeth Allen	March 17, 1896
Hives, Henry	1867
Law, Caroline	1873
Rimington, Ellen	1865
Screen, Fiona Ruth	October 22, 1967
Screen, Harry Ernest	January 27, 1892
Screen, Henry Robert	December 29, 1856
Screen, Raymond Wycherley	August 25, 1931
Southgate, Clarence William	May 13, 1894
Southgate, Patricia Helen	March 17, 1931
Southgate, William Edward	1861
Wycherley, Harry Francis	June 18, 1873
Wycherley, Mildred Dorothy	December 29, 1899

Birth Location	Death Date	Death Location
Chippenham		Sutton Scotney
Coscombe	June 17, 1965	Weymouth
Leicester	December 9, 1975	Portsmouth
Barrow		
	February 21, 1953	Shrewsbury
Market Harborough		
St Albans		
Atcham	June 6, 1972	Bath
Bristol		
Shrewsbury		
South Walsham	June 15, 1973	Portsmouth
Alfredton		
Tendiring		Sutton Scotney
	December 2, 1932	Atcham
Shrewsbury	June 1983	Bath

As you'll see from the website, there is far more to Family Treemaker than a drawing tool. It actually allows you to search for ancestors in much the same way as FamilySearch or **www.genealogy.com**, and is linked to these and other websites. It also includes something called the World Family Tree, which is a huge database of currently over 140 million names contributed by family-tree researchers all over the world. You can add your details and get in touch with other researchers by downloading the World Family Tree (for a fee).

Other popular packages for creating your tree, all of which work in much the same way as Family Treemaker, are Generations Grande Suite, Family Origins and Brother's Keeper. All are available from S&N Genealogy Services (see above for address).

Other ways of presenting your tree

One variation on the family tree you may come across is known as the indented pedigree. This is one of the ways trees are displayed on the IGI and is in a text rather than diagrammatic form. An indented pedigree for Harry Ernest Screen would look like this:

Drawing your family tree

Harry Ernest Screen who married Mildred Dorothy Wycherley in 1928 leaving issue:

1. Raymond Wycherley Screen, born 1931, married Patricia Helen Southgate in 1964 leaving issue:

> **1.** Heather Elizabeth Screen, born 1965, married José-Luis Parody in 1991 leaving issue:
>
>> **1.** Francesca Helen Parody, born 1988
>> **2.** Roseanna Marie Parody, born 2001
>
> **2.** Fiona Ruth Screen, born 1967

This can be a useful way of presenting information, but can be quite difficult to negotiate if there are a large number of children. In such cases, brothers and sisters can in fact be physically a long way apart on the page.

A concentric circle chart is another option. In this type of tree your ancestors' entries flow around yours in concentric circles. If you are the inner circle, then the surrounding circle is divided into two for your parents' details, the third circle split into four, for your grandparents' details, etc. This is quite a fun way of drawing your tree, but perhaps not the easiest to digest visually. In addition, if you have quite a few gaps in one particular line of your tree, then a rather large portion of the circle chart can look dissatisfying by blank.

If you must do it yourself…

There's no denying the pleasure that can be gained from drawing your tree by hand. I think that a lot of researchers, once they get to the stage at which they can put pen to paper, feel that letting a computer program create their tree is rather an anti-climax.

If you want to tackle a hand-drawn tree, this is what you need:

- A neat and attractive hand – if you've had some calligraphy lessons, even better
- Lots of sheets of rough paper
- A ruler
- An eraser
- All the facts to hand

Here's a tree created by one of my second cousins.

This is not a bad attempt at a tree. It's typewritten rather than hand-drawn but many of the same principles apply.

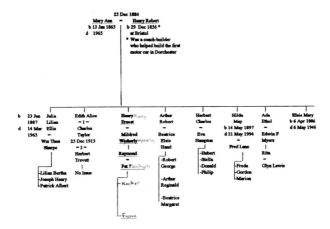

It's easy to see from this tree why a non-electronic presentation can be so difficult. One of the main problems with this tree is that relations of the same generation do not always line up. Lack of space has meant that individuals with long names have run on to two or even three lines, and therefore alignment goes to pot. This can make it seem that people of the same generation are in fact a generation apart. For example, William Thos. Sharpe in the first column looks on first glance as though he is the same generation as Raymond in the third column, but in fact he is Raymond's uncle. The same applies to Fred Lano in column six.

On this tree surnames are not given, except for Henry Robert Screen. Again, lack of space is the reason, but this causes difficulty as you have to keep searching up and down the tree to find the surname of a particular individual. For example, Julia Lilian Ellis should really be written Julia Lilian Ellis Screen.

Although a large number of drafts of this tree will have been made before the typewritten version, this tree is still very much in development. You can see that there are many dates missing, and other relations have had to fill in missing names and correct misspellings. Nevertheless, it is neat and, for a typewritten tree, relatively easy on the eye. If you try a hand-drawn or typewritten tree yourself you'll soon realize that, despite its faults, this is actually quite a successfully presented tree!

The Final Flourish

As efficient and straightforward as family-tree software programs are to use, you could be forgiven for feeling the end result is a bit of an anti-climax. You want to give the fruits of your research pride of place on your living room wall, but a piece of A4 paper with a load of names on it somehow just doesn't quite do the trick. Printing on coloured paper might help . . . but not much.

Don't worry, there are plenty of entrepreneurial types out there who have anticipated your disappointment.

The services available range from fine art creations on beautiful parchment to the lurid and frankly tacky. Most of the main genealogy websites will offer presentation services, or will have links to such companies. You can have your tree framed, mounted, gilt-edged, embossed, inscribed with your family crest or coat of arms, created in your hand-picked calligraphic script. And on it goes.

Ancestry is, unsurprisingly, often presented as carved or engraved on a tree – the imposing and sturdy oak seems to be the overall favourite. I found a website **www.troupart.com** that offers a presentation tree on

22 x 34in sepia parchment, with an attractive hand-drawn oak that holds up to seven generations in boxes on its branches. This is fairly typical of the designs available.

Another, at **www.ancestree.com**, offers a photo-montage of your ancestors on a walnut plaque, against a map of the area your family is from. I'm not sure about the map thing – it's just one flourish too many – but it's a popular idea and photographic trees can be attractive. Most of the main genealogy sites take you to a range of presentation services. Have a look around – there's some good stuff available. You might want to draw the line at mugs, place mats, T-shirts and socks with your ancestors' faces on. But if you want them, they're out there.

However you choose to present your tree, it will be a permanent reminder of why you decided to delve into your family history, and of all the things you have learnt. It will be a testament to your struggles and frustrations, to the visits to previously unknown family members, to trips to villages, churches and graveyards, and to long searches at records offices and libraries. Hopefully it will also give you a sense of place and identity, a sense of yourself as part of a bigger whole, and inspire further research.

FURTHER
READING

Amanda Bevan (ed.), *Tracing Your Ancestors in the Public Record Office*, PRO, London, 1999.

Robert Blatchford (ed.), *Family and Local History Handbook* (5th ed.), York, 2001.

Ruth Finnegan, Michael Drake, Jacqueline Eustace, *Sources and Methods for Family and Community Historians*, Cambridge University Press, Cambridge, 1997.

David Hawgood, *Internet for Genealogy*, FFHS Publications, Bury, 1999.

Mark D. Herber, *Ancestral Trails*, Sutton, Stroud, 1997.

David Hey, *The Oxford Guide to Family History*, Oxford Paperbacks, Oxford, 1998.

David Hey, *Family Names and Family History*, Hambledon & London, London, 2001.

Cecil R. Humphery-Smith (ed.), *The Phillimore Atlas and Index of Parish Registers*, Phillimore & Co Ltd, Chichester, 1995.

Roger Kershaw, Mark Pearsall, Colin Holmes, *Immigrants and Aliens*, PRO, London, 2000.

Caroline Peacock, *The Good Web Guide Genealogy*, The Good Web Guide, London, 2000.

R. Polls, *Dating Old Photographs*, Federation of Family History Societies, (2nd ed.), Bury, 1995.

Public Record Office, *Using Census Returns,* PRO Pocket Guides to Family History, London, 2000.

Colin D. Rogers, *The Family Tree Detective* (3rd ed.), Manchester University Press, Manchester, 1997.

Notes